I Should've Known Better

Nothing Lasts Forever

by

Nisha L.

Temptations
PUBLICATIONS

Email: authoressnishal@gmail.com

Website: http://www.smplygorjs.com

Facebook: www.facebook.com/AuthorSmplyGorjs

This is a fictional novel and all characters and situations in this book are a work of fiction. Any resemblances are strictly coincidental.

First Edition

Printed in the United States of America

Nonfictional/ Urban/ Drama/ Entertainment/ African American Fiction

1

Acknowledgements

I want to start by thanking GOD for blessing me the passion to write and the wonderful gift of literacy that I am now able to share with the world. We all know the saying, without him, there would be no me. I want to thank my loving husband for always encouraging me to do my best and to believe in myself. He has shown nothing but love and support the whole way through and for that I am grateful. I want to thank my mom and dad for giving me life. I thank my mom for always loving me so freely and showing me that you can overcome anything. I thank my dad for never cutting any corners; and always going the extra mile for his baby. I can always count on him to tell me what I need to know and not just what I want to hear. My mom and dad have not only taught me, but they have shown me in more ways than one, to never give up and this book is a living testimony that I am still pushing. I want to thank my grandmother and grandfather for always being in my corner; right or wrong, good or bad, they have always had my back. They taught me that it is okay to make mistakes as long as you learn from them. I want to thank my sister and my brothers for being an intricate part of my life. Although you all can really get under my skin at times, there isn't anything I wouldn't do for either or you. I want to thank my aunts and uncles for always lending an ear and encouraging words. I would like to thank all of my family, friends, and associates for their love and support throughout this journey. I am unable to list you all but please know that I am grateful to have you in my life...I love you all!

DEDICATIONS

Most people just go with the flow of life. Some are beat up along the way and some become successful. I am actively striving to be on the latter end, in hopes of making things a little bit easier for my kids along the way. Everything I do, I do with them in mind. I know that if anyone will appreciate my hard work and dedication, it's those two. I don't mind working hard or staying up late to meet deadlines. Those are small things to a giant and I will go to the end of the earth and back for you both. Marcus and London, mommy loves you both to pieces.

Table of Contents

Prologue

Sky

The rest of the trip flew by like a blizzard. We'd spent our time dining at the fanciest restaurants, shopping at some of the most exclusive boutiques that Dubai had to offer, and making out on the beach under the stars like a couple of kids. We frequented the beaches and went sightseeing in areas that even the rich and famous dreamed about.

I'd really enjoyed myself and, believe it or not, Julius and I hadn't had sex the entire time that we'd been here. We'd managed to stay busy and keep one another company without being too physical. Now don't get me wrong because there had actually been quite a few times where I'd tried to seduce him, but he wasn't having that shit. I was still having a hard time understanding how a nigga could be bricked up and still tell a baby like me no!

When I questioned his intentions, he said some shit about not wanting it to always have to result to sex with us. He said that he wanted to be able to make love to my mind, and he'd been doing just that. I never knew that I could be stimulated mentally the way that he had been doing it over the last few days.

I figured on the last night, we had no choice but to go out with a bang. And a bang it was.

He made love to me so good, I was seeing stars; and even when he was finished, my body was still tingling from his touch. Satisfied was an understatement. I mean, I thought I that I had something with Aston but the way that Julius had built me up over the past few days, taking me on an emotional roller coaster and finishing me off like I was a character in the video game *Mortal Kombat,* was crazy.

We'd connected on more than a sexual level. We connected mentally and emotionally as well, and that meant more to me than any bond that I'd ever shared with Aston.

~~~

It was close to two months after we'd made it back from Dubai before I'd finally found enough courage to break it off with Aston.

Julius and I had been spending so much time together that I hadn't had a chance to visit my bestie like I used to, let alone had time to keep playing games and stringing Aston along. So because I hadn't had time to physically go over there, I had to call him on the phone.

I was kind of thankful for that excuse because it seemed like every time I built up enough courage to break it off with him face-to-face, it was a losing battle and we'd always end up somewhere in a double tuck buck; with me yelling out in pleasure and him fucking my brains out.

I can still remember the conversation like it was yesterday. As soon as Julius left the house one night after dinner and I had a little free time to myself, the first thing I did was call Aston up. He answered on the first ring like he'd been waiting for my call.

"What's good, baby girl? Ah nigga been missing the fuck out yo lil sexy ass."

I immediately started blushing as I gave myself a pep talk. "Sky, get yo shit together, bitch! This ain't even that kind of party. Think about Julius…how would he feel?" I had to keep reminding myself that I was in love with Julius and that Aston was no good for me, but he wasn't making it any easier because he was laying it on thick as hell.

"You know, the whole time you were out of town, ah nigga couldn't stop thinking about yo ass. Now you come back and ah nigga can count on one hand how many times you done came through. I know you been busy with all of your college tours and shit, but you gotta start squeezing ya man in a lil bit more. How you gonna have ah nigga on punishment and he not even know why?" he asked, laughing.

"Ain't nobody got you on punishment. You been getting it every time I see you. How much more you want it?"

"Shittt, more than what I'm getting from you; that's for sure," he chuckled. "Sky...you betta be glad I love--"

This is where I had to draw the line before he slipped back over to home plate. "Aston, please," I interjected, cutting him off. "Don't make this harder on me that what it already is."

"What da hell you talkin--"

I quickly cut him off once more. "Just listen," I said while talking a deep breath. "You know that I love you. I'm just not sure if I'm still in love with you, and I think that it would be best if we just did our own thing for a while. I mean, if it's meant, we'll find our way back to one another…right?"

"Sky, what da fuck you talkin' bout, ma?"

"Aston, we can still be friends…I just--"

"Skyla! Are you fucking serious right nah? Fuck is up, ma? Oh, I know what it is. You must got you another nigga or something, huh? Is that what it is?" he asked as his voice cracked.

"He has nothing to do with this. I had to do this for me, Aston."

"Oh, so there is another nigga, huh? You mean to tell me dat you leave, come back and now it's over…just like that? Yo triflin' ass probably wasn't even visiting colleges. As a matter of a fact, what fucking college did you say you were visiting again?"

"I, umm…well…" He'd caught my ass slipping and I didn't have shit to say.

"That's what da fuck I thought. Ole lying ass hoe!"

"Now you wait one damn minute, Aston! I am not a hoe; and did yo punk ass forget that you cheated on me first? And you got the bitch pregnant?" I was now yelling to the top of my lungs as tears and snot dripped from my face.

"First off, that bitch ain't pregnant...and second, so what? Yea, I fucked up, but shit, I'm ah nigga. That's just what da fuck we do...but yo ass...you a female...and you was supposed to be my lady!

Silence.

"Oh, so you don't have shit to say now, huh? Can I buy a fuckin' vowel?" he yelled through the phone. "Wait! You know what? Y'all two muthafuckas can have one anotha! I don't even know what da hell I'm ova here stressing for! I don't owe yo ass shit. Talking bout we can be friends. Bitch, please...FUCK A FOREVER PIECE!" he yelled, hanging up the phone in my ear as I broke down in tears.

The conversation invaded my thoughts repeatedly as I hugged the porcelain god, empting the contents of the breakfast that I'd had with Julius this morning into the toilet.

I'd been throwing up non-stop for about three weeks now. Not to mention my period was about a week and a half late. Normally that wouldn't bother me because I'd been irregular since I first started my period back in middle school, but the fact that I couldn't keep shit down gave me pause.

Once I was finished barfing up my insides, I stood to my feet and made my way over to the sink to rinse my mouth out so that I could build up enough courage to call up my gynecologist to confirm what the other four pregnancy test had already assured me of.

My only issue is going to be breaking the news to not only Julius, who thought that he was the only one getting this candy, but also to Aston whom I'd tossed away like yesterday's trash as soon as I felt that something better had come along.

This is some real live thot shit!

Chapter One

Sky

As I sat in the corner of the waiting room with my hoodie pulled down over my head and my eyes hiding behind a pair of shades, I continued to keep my head buried in the magazine that I had picked up from the shelf when I first checked in. Anything to keep me busy because I was a nervous wreck. I'd been up all night, crying and thinking of different scenarios of how I would break the news to Julius once the doctor confirmed what I already knew to be true. In all honesty, I didn't need any confirmation. I guess I was here more so for support and alternatives.

Crazy, huh? I should have been going to Rayne for that, but with the way that I had been acting towards her lately, I wasn't sure if she still wanted be friends with me or not.

I mean, we went from being besties and sharing everything known to man to me creeping behind her back, lying, cheating on her brother, and us hardly ever seeing one another in such a short period of time. "I have to make it right with her if no one else," I sat thinking to myself.

I sulked in my seat as I thought about Julius and just what in the hell I was supposed to tell him. *"Um, hey, babe. I love you but I still have feelings for another nigga and have been going back and forth between the two of you, and now I'm pregnant and don't know which of you is the father of my child."* That's some bullshit! I couldn't do that. Julius would probably break my damn neck and Aston had already made it clear that he didn't want anything to do with my ass.

"Ms. Banks?" the nurse said, calling my name from the hall and snapping me out of my thoughts.

"That would be me," I said as I quickly stood to my feet. I made my way over to the nurse, all while doing a brief sweep of the room with my eyes, making sure that no one was watching me.

I had become so damn paranoid that it was ridiculous. But let's face it, the last thing that I needed was for someone to see me in here and go running their mouth.

"Right this way, ma'am."

I followed the nurse closely until we reached the middle of the hallway. She stopped in front of the door before holding her hand out for me to enter first. I crossed over the threshold and turned to face her just in time to see her pull a chair up and take a seat.

"Have a seat, Ms. Banks," she said as she motioned to the examination table before continuing. "So, tell me what brings you in today."

I sat down on the edge of the examination table as I watched her flip through the pages on her clipboard for a few seconds before I started to answer her. "I think...ummm...well, I took a test and it shows that..." I was at a loss for words and for some reason I couldn't even formulate a complete sentence. I was embarrassed.

She looked at me over the brim of her wire framed glasses while giggling aloud a little. "Ms. Banks, it's okay. There's no need to be nervous. We are going to take good care of you. Are you trying to say that you think that you may be pregnant?"

I blushed. "Yes, ma'am. I believe so."

"Okay, well that's not so bad. I'm gonna have you to urinate in this cup and we'll get you checked out and on your way."

"That sounds painless enough."

"You have no idea," she replied as she stood from the chair and walked over to the counter area to retrieve a specimen cup from the cabinet above the sink. She then grabbed a marker from the cup on the counter and wrote my name on the front of the cup. "Here you go, take this" she said, handing me a wipe and specimen cup. "I need you to provide a urine sample, and be sure to wipe front to back. Fill this cup up to the middle line, or as close to it as you can possibly get."

"Okay. I should be able to do that with no problem seeing as how I've been using the restroom like crazy lately," I mumbled barely above a whisper.

"Alrighty, Ms. Banks," she said as she cleared her throat and forced a smile. "Go out the door, hook a right and just follow the blue arrows until they end; they'll lead you directly to the restroom. Once you finish, open the bathroom mirror and leave your cup there."

I didn't reply. I left the room and did I was told, first following the arrows to my destination. Once I finished with the sample, I made my way back to the room and retired to the seat that the nurse had been previously sitting in. Noticing that the room was empty, my mind started to wander and once again, my thoughts were running wild.

I had pretty much moved in with Julius once we came back from Dubai so it would be pretty damn hard to hide this from him for too much longer. Last night I'd stayed over at Nana's so that I wouldn't have to explain to him where in the hell I was going this early in the morning on a Saturday. But there was no way that I was gonna miss this appointment. I had waited long enough and they only scheduled appointments up until ten o'clock in the mornings on Saturdays. Getting up at seven o'clock to make an eight thirty appointment way on the other side of town was not something that I wanted to have to do while trying to explain to him where I was going and why.

I was so caught up in my thoughts that I didn't even notice that the nurse had come back into the room until she started talking.

"Congratulations, Ms. Banks!!!! It looks like you are going to be a new mommy sometime in the near future," she expressed with too much excitement.

Once I heard those words leave her mouth, I was in total shock and disbelief. I could see her lips moving but I couldn't make out what she was saying. It was kind of like a classroom scene from *Charlie Brown*, as everything started to move in slow motion. My head was spinning and I felt myself getting lightheaded.

"Ms. Banks...Ms. Banks...hellllooooooo," I finally heard her say while waving her hand in my face to snap me out of my trance.

"Um, yes. I'm sorry..."

She laughed it off. "Oh no, don't be. It's okay. I know a thing like this can come as a big shock, especially when you're not expecting it. So I guess that means that you didn't hear me, huh?

"No ma'am. Do you mind repeating yourself?"

"Sure. Not a problem. Could you please disrobe from the waist down and lay on the examination table. You can place this across your lower half once you're finished. I'm gonna step out to give you a little privacy. I'll be back in shortly with the doctor."

"Oh...umm...okay...and what's this for?"

"Your test came back positive and we have to see how far along you are, sweetie," she said as she made her way out the door.

I sat there for a few minutes in total shock before I was able to let the confirmation sink it. I slowly started to do as I was told and somewhere in between taking off my clothes and the doctor coming into the room, I guess I had climbed up onto the examination table because when I came to, I was lying flat on my back with my knees facing the ceiling and an older Indian guy was sitting on a small stool at the foot of the table, telling me to place my feet in the stirrups and to bring my bottom down to the edge of the table.

I immediately tensed up until I looked to my right and saw that the nurse was still there. I guess her job was to make sure everything stayed professional from this point on. I loosened up a little and did as I was told.

"So, Ms. Banks, is it?"

"Yes," I mumbled barely above a whisper.

"When was your last menstrual cycle?"

I started thinking to myself, trying to figure out when I'd had my last period, and I kept coming up empty. I remember it coming on before Dubai, but that had been at least three months ago.

"I can't say that I remember."

"No problem. That's what I'm here for anyhow," he said, smiling up at me as he looked over the brim of his glasses and reached over to grab a pair of gloves from the little table that the nurse had prepped for him.

Once he put the gloves on, he reached over, grabbed a white tube and flipped the cap back. While squeezing the contents from the tube onto his fingers, he took a moment to finally introduce himself. Shit, that's something he should have done when he first came in. But hell, I was so out of it, I probably wouldn't have even heard him anyway.

"By the way, I'm Dr. Nassir. I'll be filling in for your primary physician, Dr. Lacey, while she's out on maternity leave. So if you have any questions or concerns that you'd like to discuss, feel free to do so."

He placed his left hand right in the space above my pubic area and just below the bottom of my stomach. "This may be a little cold," he said as he slowly guided his right hand into my opening, using what felt like two fingers. He pressed down on my stomach in the process, as he maneuvered his fingers around in my insides.

"Hmm. Okayyyy," he mumbled more to himself than anything else.

"Hmm, what?" I immediately started to panic. "What's wrong, doctor?" I asked, now lifting my head from the table and trying to sit up at the same time.

"Oh no, sweetie. Everything is fine," the nurse said as she gently placed her hand on my shoulder. "Lay back down."

I reluctantly laid back down, but not quietly. "Doctor, can you tell me what's going on?"

I wasn't ready for any kids and definitely hadn't planned on having any so soon, but the last thing I wanted was for something to be wrong with my baby. I guess my motherly instincts kicked in immediately because I was ready for some answers.

"I'm sorry if I alarmed you, Ms. Banks. It's just that normally, first prenatal visits are scheduled within the first eight to ten weeks of pregnancy, and from this pelvic exam, it seems that you may actually be a little further along than just a couple of weeks," he said as he removed his gloves and placed them into the waste basket.

"Oh?" I asked more as a question than anything else. "Well, exactly how far along am I?"

"That I'm not sure of. We're going to have to do an ultrasound to determine that. Don't worry. It's painless and it'll only take about 10 minutes or so."

I let out a sigh as I stared up at the ceiling, allowing Dr. Nassir to do his job. He squirted something cool on my stomach and turned the monitor on as he probed my belly, pressing down in certain spots.

I looked at the small screen and saw what looked like a little half-developed alien. I couldn't make out all of the features, but there was definitely something there.

I think that's when everything started to register. I was really about to be someone's mother. Tears immediately started pouring from my eyes as my heart became flooded with a mix of emotions. I was happy, sad, scared and excited all at the same time; but my tears were definitely tears of joy as I came to the realization that there was a life growing inside of me that would depend on me for everything.

"Well, Ms. Banks, everything looks good. The baby is developing well and right on schedule. The heartbeat is strong and I've only seen signs of a healthy baby thus far."

"That's good. Were you able to tell how far along I am?"

"Of course. You are exactly three months and four days to date. That will put you right around September 27 for delivery. Now keep in mind that this date may change with time, depending on the baby and, of course, your health."

I nodded my head, signaling that I understood as he continued.

"Now I'm going to write you a prescription for your prenatal pills and you can schedule your next appointment with the receptionist on your way out."

"An appointment for what?" I asked skeptically.

He chuckled a little like something was funny before answering. "You will have to come in at least once a month to make sure that the baby is developing okay and that everything is moving according to schedule; and closer to the date, the amount of check-ups per month will increase as well because we have to not only make sure that the baby is doing okay, but we also have to make sure that you stay healthy as well."

"Okay, that makes sense," I mumbled.

"Your prescription will be at the front waiting, and you can go ahead and get dressed now as well. I'll see you again next month, Ms. Banks," he spoke as he let himself out of the room with the nurse following close behind.

Chapter Two

Aston

Baby I love you

You are my life

My happiest moments weren't complete

If you weren't by my side

The sweet melody of Beyoncé's "Dangerously in Love 2" woke me out of my sleep smiling, but when I remembered Skyla assigned that as her ringtone the last time we were together, it made my skin crawl.

Wondering what the hell she wanted, I hesitated to pick up. I'd been dodging her calls for quite some time now. Hell, she broke up with me but won't stop calling. What the hell do we need to talk about at this point? She shoulda been talking before the breakup.

The phone soon stopped ringing so I turned back over to go back to sleep and it started again. Same lyrics and same song, but for some reason, the ring tone seemed to only get louder and louder with each syllable that Beyoncé sang.

Getting aggravated, I angrily swiped my finger across the screen of my phone, accepting the call just as it was about to roll over to voicemail for the second time.

"Why in the hell do you keep cycle dialing me, Skyla?"

Silence.

"Hello? Hellooooo…I know it's you. Your shit is still programmed in my phone, you know?" I asked sarcastically into the phone.

"Aston, we need to talk," she said meekly.

"We don't have shit to talk about and you made sure of that."

"Aston, please. It's really important. Can we meet somewhere to talk?"

"Hell nah. I ain't tryna see you dawg, so you know what that means? It means that anything that you want to talk to me about, you can talk to me over the phone." I was fuming hot that this chick had the audacity to even think that it was okay for her to call my phone on some ole rah-rah shit like we're friends or something; "And you need to make this shit quick too because I got shit to do," I spat into the phone for good measure.

I could hear her sniffling on the other end of the phone, and as much as it broke my heart, I couldn't let her know that she still had ah nigga in her pocket so I just played it cool and waited for her to respond.

"Fine! Since you wanna be like that, I just called to tell you that I'm pregnant."

"Okay, annndddd?" I asked, not following her rendition of a story.

"Watchu mean, 'Okay and'? This could very well be yo' baby, Aston."

"Humph...is that your final answer?"

"Fuck you, Aston! You got some nerve. How are you just gonna treat me like some hoe off of the street? You got me fucked up. Here I am trying to be a woman and tell you that this may be your child and here you go showing your ass! I can't stand you!" she yelled into the phone.

"You know what, Sky? Muthafuck you! Talking about you tryna be a woman. Yo' ass wasn't being a woman about yo' shit when you couldn't come tell me that you was feeling anotha nigga. Yo' ass wasn't being a woman when you was out sucking beach balls through straws and fucking that nigga sideways, giving up what was supposed to be reserved for me. But now you want me to believe that because you pregnant and telling me that I may possibly have a child on the way that you're being a woman about yours? Nah, baby girl, it don't work like that!

"Let's not get this shit twisted. You're not being a woman, you're being a hoe; and as a matter of a fact, yo' ass is no better at it than Kia. Hell, and just being a hunnit, she may be mo' A1 than you because at least she knew that if she was pregnant, it would have been by me. Yo' ass just winging it and hoping for the best because you know that deep down I'm a good dude. I may have fucked up but you know my shit was certified and I've always been upfront with you. Now get off my phone and go call the nigga that you've been fucking behind my back for the last few months and tell his ass that I said congratulations because I don't want shit to do with you and I damn sholl don't want nothing to do with anotha nigga's seed!" I said, laughing. "Sheeiiitttt, and I bet he think he got himself something," I said before hanging up the phone in her ear.

I was so calm that I'd scared myself. "That bitch got the right one nah," I thought to myself. The ball was definitely in my court.

Knock! Knock! Knock!

"Well I'll be damned," I thought to myself as I listened to my door rattle.

"Aston! Open this damn door! I know that you're in there!"

"Raye, leave me the hell alone. I'm tired and I don't feel like being bothered."

"That's a damn lie. Your ass ain't tired. Shit, you ain't been doing nothing but sleeping for the last few weeks anyway. So even if yo ass was tired, you should be well rested by now. Hell, if I didn't know any better, I'd say that your ass been in hibernation!" she yelled while laughing from the other side of the door.

"That shit ain't funny, Raye! A nigga just ain't feeling up to having any company right now. I just wanna be by myself. I need to figure some things out," I said as I walked over to the door and unlocked it.

She immediately opened the door, staring at me like she was ready to tell my ass a thing or two.

"Wassup? Why you looking at me like that?"

"Because, nigga! I know that something is wrong with yo' ass, so just spill it."

"Nah, ain't nothing wrong. I'm straight."

"I thought we were better than that. You been walking around here, looking all ugly in the face, not eating, and you haven't even been hanging out like you used to. Shit, this ain't like you! Let me guess," she said, leaning against the door frame and crossing her arms. "You and Sky must be going through it?"

I looked at her carefully for the first time since she'd been standing in the doorway and realized that she had no clue about what was going on. I was thankful that she hadn't heard the argument that Sky and I had just had because I knew that she would have been pissed.

"You mean to tell me that Sky ain't already gave you a play-by-play?"

"A play-by-play of what? I haven't spoken to Sky in almost a month, with the exception of a few text messages here and there. We just agreed last night to hang out tomorrow since we haven't had the time to chill with one another lately."

"Humph."

"Humph, what? What the hell happened? Did I miss something?"

"I'll letcha girl give you the run down, but just for the record, we're not together anymore."

"What the…when did…Aston, are you serious?"

"As a heart attack, sis," I replied as I gently pushed her away from the doorway, closing and locking my door behind her.

I could tell by the look on her face that she really had no clue about what was going on between Sky and I. I guess her ass was too damned embarrassed to say anything. Shit, I mean, what in the hell can she say with her foul ass?

I can't even front though, I still love her, but ah nigga ain't finna be nobody's fool.

"Who woulda ever thought that my forever piece would shit on ah nigga like this?" I asked aloud as I chuckled to myself. "Boy, how the tables have turned."

Mama always told me that you reap what you sow and I never really bought into that shit, but now ah nigga can see this shit coming full circle.

I guess I just gotta count my blessing because it could definitely be worse. I still got life and it's time for me to start acting like it. Hell, this ain't the end of the world and Sky's ass damn sholl ain't the only bitch on the planet.

I picked up my phone and dialed Allison's number. I hadn't spoken to her in months but I knew that her ass would be happy to hear from ah nigga…and I won't even have to ask her to come through to tighten me up because she gon' do dat anyway.

"Hey, you!" she answer, sounding a little too hyped.

"Wassup witcha? You busy?"

"Not really. I was about to go to catch me a matinee, unless you want some company, of course."

"It's alright, ma, if you already have plans, ah nigga can holla atcha later."

"Ain't no telling how long from now that will be, so you can cancel that shit," she said laughing. "I'm busting a U right now!"

I clicked the end button and chuckled to myself. "Yep, ya boy still got it."

Chapter Three

Sky

As I stood at the stove preparing dinner for Julius and me, I couldn't stop the tears from flowing from my eyes. I didn't know how I was gonna break the news about the pregnancy to him.

I kept going over different scenarios in my head of how I could tell him, but each time I came up empty. I didn't know how in the hell I got myself caught up in this bullshit.

I wanted to be happy because GOD was blessing me with my own little bundle of joy, but I couldn't help but to be sad.

Here I was with my whole life ahead of me, and now a bomb like this? What in the hell was I gonna do with a baby? Hell, I'm just learning how to take care of myself, and not even that because Julius does that for the most part, and right behind him is Nana and Granddaddy.

"Damn, boo. You got it smelling good as hell up in here."

I'd been so caught up in my thoughts that I hadn't even heard Julius walk in. I hurried and dried my eyes because I knew that he was on his way over to hug and kiss me. That was our thing. Anytime he left or came in, we made sure to kiss one another.

True to form, he made his way over to the stove and wrapped his arms around me from behind, kissing the side of my cheek.

Acting surprised, I gasped. "Hey, youuuu!" I said, turning around to peck him on the lips. "Are you hungry?"

"I didn't think that I was, but after smelling the food on the stove, I could probably eat a little bit."

"Good! Because I cooked one of your favorites," I said smiling.

"And what would that be?"

"Chicken alfredo, garlic bread and I threw together a salad."

"Word? That's wassup."

I pecked his lips once more before turning around to check the food. "Go ahead and get situated, bae. It's almost done."

"Alright, I can see you didn't wait for me tonight so I'm gonna go hop in the shower and I'll be back down to eat in a few."

"Okay. That's cool."

"Unn huh…and be ready to talk when I come back down," he said as he turned to walk off.

I immediately tensed up. I could feel the butterflies start to flutter in my stomach and my heart as it started to beat faster and faster by the second.

The first thing that came to mind is that someone had seen me at the doctor's office, or that somehow he had figured out that I was pregnant. I had been really careful lately, making sure that he stayed unaware of my new state.

Scared to ask, but dying to know, I managed to ask anyhow. "Talk about what, bae?"

He continued walking until he reached the bottom of the stairs before turning to answer me. "About why you standing in there crying. You know I can tell when something is wrong with you, Sky. You beautiful but you look like shit right now," he said, laughing.

I immediately got defensive. "Go to hell, JuJu!" I yelled while rolling my eyes and turning my back to him.

"Man, calm down, woman. I didn't mean it like that. I just meant that usually when I come home, you're prancing around in some kind of lil nightie that's barely covering ya ass while you're cooking. Now don't get me wrong because ah nigga love that shit, but today I come home and you in here in my basketball shorts and tank top, and you rocking my damn bath robe!" He was now laughing like a hyena as he continued, "And hell, we ain't even gonna start on that damn head wrap you got on. Shit, I thought you had done let ah nigga up in this bitch when I first walked in."

"Ha ha...not funny," I said, folding my arms and turning back to look at him.

He was laughing so hard, he *looked* like a damn hyena.

"I'm glad that you're amused," I said, now growing impatient with his black ass.

"All I'm saying is that something has got to be wrong for me to come home and my baby in here looking like one of the boys."

I was now smiling at how goofy he was being. This was one of the things that I loved about him. He was always able to make me smile.

"There we go," he said, pointing. "I just wanted to see you smile, beautiful. But seriously, your face is all red and your eyes are all puffy and swollen. You look like you been in here blowing strong, bae! Shit, as a matter of a fact," he said as he started jogging up the stairs, "let me go check my damn stash!" he yelled behind him.

I couldn't do nothing but laugh. I couldn't stand his ass but I loved him to death. I just didn't know how much longer I'd be able to keep up the charade.

~~~

We sat the table eating and making small talk and I couldn't be happier. I knew that he hadn't forgotten about it because this nigga didn't forget shit! I just didn't want to have to lie tonight. But I knew that he wasn't gonna let me off that easy and I had it all mapped out in my mind what I would say whenever he decided to ask. I just wished that there was a better way.

"Why are you so quiet?"

"Shit, I was waiting to see if you was gonna tell ah nigga what all the tears were for earlier today, but since it seems like you not gonna take the bait, I guess I'll just have to ask. What was wrong with you earlier?"

Because I'd already mentally prepared myself for this conversation, I jumped right in without missing a beat. "Nothing serious, bae. I was just thinking about everything that Ty and I have been through over the last few years. You know, some people go through things and they aren't able to bounce back. I'm just glad that I wasn't one of them."

Julius looked at me, nodding his head up and down. "I don't know how many times I've gotta tell you, Sky, you're made of some real special shit, baby!"

"I know. I just gotta start believing that myself."

"Oh, you will, and I'll be right here with you every step of the way."

I breathed a sigh of relief. I'd definitely dodged a bullet tonight. I'd have to be more careful in the future. "I love you, JuJu."

"I love you too, beautiful… Now let's go upstairs so you can show me just how much you love me," he said, getting up from the table.

"Right behind you, daddy," I cooed, leaving the table just as it was and following suit.

Chapter Four

Sky

"Hey, Sky. What's up? Are you outside?"

"Is your brother there?"

"Nah, his ass finally left about twenty minutes ago. Why? What's wrong?"

"Nothing. I just didn't want to chance seeing him, that's all. I'm pulling in your driveway now."

"Okay, cool. I'll be out, let me grab my purse and lock up."

As I sat waiting on Raye to make it outside, I thought about all of the good times that Aston and I had had together, and I desperately wanted to reach out to him but maybe it was still a little too soon. Hell, the last time I talked to him, I distinctively remember him hating my guts, and I'm pretty damn sure that not much had changed since then.

"What's up, chick?" Raye squealed as she hopped into the passenger seat, buckling her seatbelt.

"Not a damn thing!" I replied, smiling, and realizing just how much I'd missed my friend.

It's not every day that you find real friends and that's exactly what Raye had been to me for as long as I could remember, so I had every intention of making shit right between us.

"Soooo, where are we off to?"

"I don't know. I thought that you had something in mind."

"Me? Hell, last night on the phone, you made it clear that you didn't want to chill at the house, so I figured yo ass would have our day all mapped out."

I shrugged my shoulders and laughed. "I guess you're right, heffa!"

"As usual," she teased. "Now, where to?"

"I guess we can do our usual and head over to the mall. It's a one stop shop because yo ass always hungry so we can grab a bite to eat and then shop until we drop, I guess."

"Sounds like a plan to me," she said, leaning forward to turn the radio up as she sang along with the lyrics from Mariah Carey's "Beautiful."

Traffic was light and it only took a few minutes for us to make it to the mall, but I guess that was because every car in the universe was here at the mall. We'd made it to the mall in record time but it took damn near a decade for us to find parking, and once we finally found a spot, it was all the way in the boondocks!

"Welp, I hope you don't have a problem with walking, Raye."

"Not at all, hunny. Besides, maybe I'll be able to turn a few heads while I'm at it!" she said, getting out of the car.

I looked at her in shock as I hopped out of the car and clicked the lock button. "What do you mean? I know I ain't been gone that damn long. You and B not together anymore?"

She looked at me like I had lost my mind or something.

"What? Why you looking at me like that?"

"Chile, please, you tried it! B ain't going nowhere!"

"Then why in the hell you tryna turn heads then?" I asked with confusion.

"Because, Sky, me and B are together all day, every day, and it just feels good to know that you still got it every now and then."

"Bitch, you know you still got it so don't even try it."

"I guess you're right," she said smiling, "but the compliments aren't the same coming from him all the time. Sometimes you just need someone else to look at you and tell you how beautiful you are. I mean, I love to hear all of those things from B, but he's my man so he's supposed to compliment me. Shoot!" she sighed while sucking her teeth.

I busted out laughing. "And to think, I'd almost forgot how much of an attention whore you are," I said jokingly.

"Well, hell, if you'd stop ditching your girl for dem niggas you tryna juggle, you wouldn't have a chance to forget," she said, sticking her tongue out at me.

"Shut up, heffa!" I was laughing so hard that I almost choked. "You know, you are so dramatic that it ain't even funny!"

"Whatever!"

"Unn huh…and what makes you think that I've been juggling niggas?" I asked, opening the door to the mall.

"Because I know yo ass, Sky, and I noticed that ever since MiMi introduced us to JuJu's ass, you've been acting hella weird and being so damn secretive."

"But that don't—"

She cut me off in mid-sentence. "Girl, bye! I'm not stupid, Sky. I put two and two together that day in the mall, so you can cut the bullshit! Besides, when Aston's ass mentioned you being away on a college tour that I knew nothing about a few months back, I immediately knew something was up. So I called MiMi and interrogated her ass until she gave me the scoop."

"How in the hell did MiMi…" Before I could even finish the question, it was like a light bulb went off in my head. "Never mind. That is JuJu's cousin, huh?" I mumbled more so to myself that anyone else. But it wouldn't have been Raye if she would have just let that slide by without digging a little.

"You damn right, that's her cousin and you know her ass can't hold water," she said laughing.

"I guess you're right. But shit, in my defense, you'd been acting real shitty with me when it came to him, and I didn't want to strain our relationship any more than I already had," I confessed truthfully.

"Awww, Sky. Girl, you ought to know by now that no matter what, I'm gonna have yo damn back. I just didn't want you jumpin out of one relationship and right into another one. We both know that my brother is an asshole, but he loves you, and that I know without a doubt. I mean, honestly, I was kind of hoping that y'all would eventually work shit out. But I guess things don't always happen the way that we'd like for them to."

Listening to Raye talk had me getting teary-eyed. I didn't know if it was my hormones that had me all choked up or if what she was saying was really just that deep.

"I know, Raye, and I love him, too. I was just so damn hurt by what he did to me that all I wanted was to get back at him. I never knew that I'd meet such a great guy in Julius and fall in love all over again." I was now walking through the mall, crying a river, and pouring my heart out all at the same damn time.

I guess it took a minute for Raye to realize that I was crying, but being the friend that she'd always been to me, she was there with a shoulder for me to lean on. She stopped walking and turned toward me, grabbed my arm in the process and led me over to the bench in the middle of the aisle. She wrapped her arms around me and hugged me for dear life as she whispered in my ear, "It's okay, Sky. Everything will be just fine."

I could barely even speak. All I could do was shake my head and cry onto her shoulder. "No it won't, Raye. He hates me! He won't even

talk to me anymore."

There wasn't much more she could say, so she just continued to rub my back and console me.

"Skyla, yes, hunny... Sshhh, it's okay. Everything will work itself out. You've been through worse, so I know that you can get through this, too."

After I felt like I just didn't have any more tears left, I was finally able to calm down a little. "Raye, you know that we've always been able to be upfront with one another, and I've never in my life had to feel the need to hide anything from you...up until a few months ago."

"Sky, it's cool. We all make mistakes; let's just start over from here."

"It's not that easy, Raye. I have some shit that I need to get off of my chest and I don't have anyone else to talk to, but because I know that I can trust you with my life, I want to tell you," I said somberly.

"Sky, you know you can tell me anything and I won't judge you, but you also know that I'm not gonna pull no punches with you either. I'm gonna give you my honest opinion about whatever it is, whether you ask for it or not."

I could see the sincerity in her eyes and I knew that if anyone would give me some sound advice, it would be her. "Well I'm definitely ready to share this load because all of this sneaking around has been beyond exhausting for me."

She looked at me and laughed.

"Whatttt? It has been!"

"Yep. I knew yo ass had been up to no good, and I guess I'm about to find out just how much shit you've been into, huh?"

I just nodded my head yes and started my purge. "Well, you already know that me and Julius have been seeing one another, and it's obvious now that I'd been going back and forth between him and Aston; but what you didn't know is that JuJu and I are an item now."

Her eyebrows rose in shock as I revealed all of my dirty little secrets; choosing to ignore her facial expressions and continue, all the while acting as if I hadn't seen the yolk on her face.

"And just as you suspected, I wasn't on a college tour. He'd actually taken me away to Dubai for my birthday, Raye; and ever since we came back, I've pretty much been staying at his place. Things were moving so fast that I didn't have time to stop and think about what was going on and how anyone else outside of me would feel."

"So you mean to tell me that you've been dating Julius for months now, and you're just now deciding to tell me?" she asked with a confused look on her face.

I held my head down as I processed her question before answering. "Yes, but like I said before, in the beginning, I had no intentions of being with Julius. He was just in the right place at the right time, and he served as a great distraction. I never knew that I'd fall in love in the process, and now I'm in too deep, Raye. I'm pretty sure that I love this man."

"I can't bel—" Before she could finish, I cut her off.

"Raye…there's more."

"Really?" she asked with sarcasm before pausing to allow me to continue.

"It wasn't long ago that I was still seeing Aston as well…and I mean seeing him, seeing him…" my voice then started to trail off as my eyes filled with water once again before continuing, "…and now I'm pregnant," I said under my breath in a barely audible tone.

It took a minute for what I was trying to tell Raye to register, but when it did, her eyes were the size of silver dollars as her mouth formed into the shape of an oval and she placed her hand over her mouth before yelling in a high pitched whisper, "Ooohhhhh, bitch! Sky, please don't tell me that this is Aston's baby!"

She was looking at me for an answer and I didn't really have one for her. Shit, I didn't know my damn self whose child I was carrying, so how in the hell did she expect for me to be able to tell her ass? I let a tear fall as I sat for a few more seconds contemplating how to go about answering her question without making myself out to be some kind of whore, but it was no use. It was what it was.

"Raye...honestly? I wish that I could tell you that this is Aston's baby that I'm carrying, but I really don't know."

"What? What the hell do you mean you don't know? Sky, come onnnnn, man. What the hell kind of shit is that?"

"Raye, I know, but to keep it all the way real with you, I was enjoying being able to have my cake and eat it too, I guess."

"Yeah, well, looks like yo ass done had too damn much cake. Have you told Julius yet?"

"No. But I've already told Aston, and that's how I know that he hates the ground that I walk on."

"Damn, Sky. I don't know how in the hell you gonna get out of this one, but you know that I'm here if you need me," she said soothingly.

"You're not pissed at me?" I asked with shock. I'd really expected Raye to rip me a new asshole once I let all of those skeletons out, but she actually did the complete opposite. I guess she could sense that I just really needed a friend more than anything right then.

"No ma'am, you got enough shit on your plate. But I will say this, if it was me, I would tell Julius sooner rather than later because you can only hide a pregnancy for so long."

"Yea, I know. I just gotta wait until the time is right to tell him. Shit, if Aston cursed me out the way that he did and we weren't even together, I can only imagine how Julius is gonna flip out on my ass."

"I'm witcha when you're right."

We sat there on the bench for another hour just catching up on everything that we'd missed in one another's lives, from my twisted love affair and the child that I was carrying to how serious she and Bryce had gotten and how she was starting to feel like she needed a break.

Raye was a live wire and she felt that he was smothering her. I guess she needed a breather. I just hoped that she talked to him about her feelings and putting some space between them before she ended up like me.

"Alright, enough about our men. Let's go grab something to eat from the Cheesecake Factory because I done talked up an appetite," I laughed.

"Awwww, TT's baby is hungryyyy," she cooed in a baby voice while rubbing my barely there stomach.

I quickly slapped her hand away, afraid that someone would see her. "Cut that shit out, Raye." I was laughing but I was dead serious. Although it was kind of cute, I wasn't ready to let the world know just yet that I'd gotten myself knocked up.

"Fine! You heffa you! Just wait until that belly gets bigger. You won't be able to keep me away from it! I can't wait until we can start shopping," she said, getting up from the bench. "Now come on so we can hurry up and eat because you know I gotta hit Macy's before we leave," she said with a smile.

Before I could even say anything, she chimed in again, "And don't even think about ditching me to go to Zara today after all of the shit that you just told me," she said, winking her eye and smiling as she led the way to the restaurant located in the front of the mall.

"You gotta love her," I thought to myself as I allowed her to lead the way like she was on a catwalk in Paris.

Chapter Five

Julius

I pulled up to the old abandoned warehouse and circled it twice before backing my car in next to a tree. I pulled my hair back into a ponytail and pulled the black ski mask down over my face.

Just as I was putting my gloves on, I noticed Skeet and Ant pulling into the parking lot, doing just as I'd done not even a few minutes prior. I watched as they circled the building twice and proceeded to park on the opposite side of the tree.

"This is it," I told myself.

I had been screaming to Sky that I would be out of the game as soon as I was able to tie up a few loose ends, and it was about time that I made good on my promises. Now that I know who the snake is in my camp, I can do just that.

I hopped out of the car and made my way to the door of the building, being careful to make sure that no one was around before inserting my key and entering. I walked into the warehouse and surveyed the premises. I could have stayed put and sent my boys to do this, but I liked to be sure of my surroundings. Although the old warehouse belonged to me and I was very familiar with it inside and out, I still had to make sure for my own sanity that everything was on the up-and-up. I didn't need any surprises.

Once I'd survey the entire warehouse and was satisfied with the sweep, I walked back over to the door and signaled for Skeet and Ant to come in. It was then that I realized that they were both in the front seat. That was a NO-NO. I dropped my head, thinking that they couldn't have been that damn stupid. "These niggas ain't new to this," I mumbled under my breath.

I hurried and waved my hand in the air, letting them know that the coast was clear. When they retired from their seats in the front of the car, Ant walked around to meet Skeet on the other side, where he stood watch as Skeet prepared to open the door.

"At least they did remember to put the child locks on," I thought to myself while shaking my head.

When they opened the back door, I was floored to see Marquise escorting Melo out of the car with a pistol.

From where I stood, it looked as if Melo was chained and shackled at the feet. I couldn't see his face because it had been covered with a potato sack. I'm guessing to prevent him from being able to see where he was going; but hell, with what I have in mind, he won't be able to use his eyes anyway. Besides, his ass won't be able to find his way back from hell, because that's exactly where his ass was going tonight.

We were out in the middle of nowhere and I knew that no one was around, but for some reason my stomach was in knots and that was something that I'd learned to pay very special attention to over the years. It was kind of like a woman's intuition, except for men.

I didn't know much about Marquise but Ant and Skeet were like brothers to me, and I knew damn well they knew that they were gonna have some problems with me when this shit is all said and done.

I watched as Ant led the way and Skeet stood behind to make sure that everything was on the up-and-up. Once we were all inside, Skeet and Ant immediately drew their guns. This was the norm for us so I could smell the revenge in the air as my blood started to boil, and the adrenaline pumped through my veins like a BOSE sound system.

I was usually a man of very few words but the longer I stood there assessing the situation, the more I wanted to know what in the hell would make Melo steal from me. I took him in off of the streets and helped him get up on his feet. I'd even bought him and his grandma a new house since that was the only family he had.

I'd been nothing but loyal and a man of my word. Hell, he'd even became like a brother to me over the last few years, and before I'd met Sky, me, him, Skeet and Ant were always together. Now this nigga done flipped the script on me. "You damn right I need answers," I thought to myself as I stepped closer to him and snatched the potato sack off of his head.

He seemed to be a little drowsy as he struggled to focus his eyes forward. Once his vision came into focus, I lifted my ski mask so that he could meet his maker before he was put to rest. His eyes bucked and he completely lost control of his bowels.

"You nasty son of a bitch!" I roared as I hauled off and slapped fire from his ass using the back of my hand.

"I'm sorry," he managed to mumble through a now busted lip as I looked at him in disgust.

"Sorry is right... You know, Melo...at one point in time, I was really fond of you...I took you under my wings...groomed you...and treated you pretty well, if I may say so myself. Now, I'd like to think that I'm a pretty fair man, wouldn't you say?"

He nodded his head weakly.

"Whenever I eat, I make sure that we all eat. I'm not greedy at all, but you," I said pointing at him, "you, my friend, your eyes just got too big for your stomach and you started to bite off more than you could chew. But I'm willing to make a deal with you...in exchange for your life, of course."

Skeet and Ant whipped their heads in my direction because it was unheard of for me to make deals. Even Marquise, who'd now dropped his pistol down at his side and focused in on me was shocked.

Melo slowly lifted his head and managed to find a little bit of hope. At least it was enough hope to respond to my offer, anyway.

"Anything, boss."

I let out an evil laugh while shaking my head up and down because I knew something that they didn't know. What I wanted would be impossible for Melo to come up with because he was young and foolish. He wasn't capable of making provisions; he was an in the moment kind of guy.

"Good! I like yo attitude, boy!" I laughed teasingly. "Now, if you can get me at least half of the mil that you've stole from me over the last three months, I'll spare your life right now," I expressed with a wicked grin as I watched the color drain from his face.

Silence.

"Well?" I asked while glaring into his eyes.

Silence.

"I didn't think so," I said, pulling my .9mm from the small of my back and aiming it at his head.

"Wait! Wait! Wait! Boss!" he yelled, trying to save his life.

"You got my muthafuckin' money, boy?" I asked with death dripping from each word.

"Boss...please," he whispered as slobber fell from his mouth.

"Do...you...have...my...mutha...fuckin'...money ...boy?" I asked once more.

"No! But, I have something better than that," he slurred with his hands up, palms facing me.

"And just what do you have for me that's better than my damn money?"

"A name," he mumbled as his eyes shifted.

"A name for what?"

"I wasn't alone, boss--"

"Mannnn, fuck this shit! This nigga is tripping!" Marquise raged, cutting him off and aiming his gun.

I could feel it in my bones. Some shit was definitely getting ready to pop off. I clutched my piece a little tighter as I glanced over and barked, cutting him off in mid-sentence, "Yo', Marquise, let the man talk!"

Skeet and Ant were posted and ready for whatever. They were taught to shoot first and ask questions later and I knew that neither of them had a problem with that.

"What the fuck do you mean, you weren't alone? You mean to tell me that you had other muthafuckas helping you take my shit?" I yelled with spittle flying from my mouth.

Silence.

"I asked you a muthafuckin' question…and why are you telling me this now all of the sudden?" I asked through clenched teeth.

Silence.

"Speak, bitch!" I roared, slapping him across the face with my gun.

It looked like something out of the movie as I watched blood spew from his mouth and his knees buckle, causing him to fall down.

"Pleaseeeeee," he begged. "I'll talk…"

It was about to be like the Wild Wild West up in this bitch and I'd planned on still being one of the very few to still be standing once the smoked cleared. I cocked my gun, putting one in the chamber. I knew that my boys and I were thinking the same thing because without a second thought, I could hear Skeet and Ant cock their guns simultaneously.

"I'm listening," I said as I tilted my head to the side to get a good look at his now swollen face as he began to speak.

"Fuck it!" he yelled. "I'm gonna die today, anyway. I know how you roll so I already know that I won't be making it out of this bitch alive."

"A very smart man you are," I said, nodding in his direction. "Just not smart enough, I guess. Otherwise we wouldn't even be here right now. So speak on it!"

He shook his head before continuing to speak. "It was him," he mumbled barely above a whisper.

I could see everyone's bodies shift and tense up; and I can't even lie, it made me cautious. I was praying that the old saying, 'keep your friends close and your enemies closer,' didn't prove to be true right now. I knew damn well this muthafucka wasn't trying to tell me that my boys, my got damn brothers, had been living foul, screwing me behind my back, and robbing me blind. I looked back and forth between Ant and Skeet, trying to make some sense of what he was saying before focusing my attention back to Melo.

"Him who?" I asked, placing the gun against his temple while looking around at the other three men standing around me. Never being one to be caught off guard, I reached down and pulled my Ruger LC9 from my sock with the other hand and trained it on the other three men standing before me. If it had to come down to life or death, my brothers wouldn't be exempt.

"Come on nah, JuJu. You know damn well that's some bullshit!" Skeet yelled.

Ant just stood there, gun still trained, but unlike Skeet's gun, which was still pointed in Melo's direction, his was now pointed at me. Much like myself, Ant was a man of very few words and, outside of the little doubt that had just been placed into my mind, his loyalty normally spoke volumes so I guess he didn't feel like he needed to explain himself. I completely understood that, but still I wasn't taking any chances.

Skeet and Ant's aims were just as good as mine and I knew that if shit got any uglier, I wouldn't be making it out of this bitch alive, but neither would they. It would be one big ass blood bath. I wasn't worried about Marquise's aim because Skeet was ready to put in work and if it came down to it, his ass won't even be able to blink before Skeet filled him with some hot shit.

Hoping to not have to go there with my boys, I looked back to Melo for answers. I needed to know what the fuck was up, and quick, because shit didn't look like it was going to get any prettier.

"He's dirty…" he gasped, trying to catch his breath. "He's been taking money…before me…his ass is…foul…Mar…quis-"

BLAOW! BLAOW! Shots sounded off as Melo's body fell to the ground before he could get the entire name out of his mouth. Marquise had put two bullets in his chest, and it immediately set off a chain reaction because before Melo could take his last breath, Skeet, Ant and I had all emptied our clips into Marquise's body.

I watched with glee as the bullets tore into his torso and blew off half of his face. I felt a sense of calm and satisfaction as brain matter and guts flew from the holes in his body and I watched as what was left of his body went limp and dropped to the floor.

Melo may not have had a chance to give us a play-by-play, but we'd heard enough to know that he wasn't the only snake in my camp. Marquise's ass was living foul and he had to go too.

Once the gun play subsided, I dropped my piece and reached into my back pocket, grabbed my hunting knife, and walked over to the still warm corpse of what used to be Melo's body. I took my time cutting off each of his fingers. I had to have a souvenir to send to his grandma; and to think, I really liked her.

When I finished, I stood up and pointed at my handy work before saying, "Be sure to take care of this."

They nodded their heads in unison because they knew exactly what to do with it.

Now I had to ease the tension between my brothers and me. It was really bothering me that I'd doubted them. I walked over to Skeet and looked him the eyes. "Shit got real tonight, and I appreciate you having my back."

"No doubt, you fam," he said, giving me our signature handshake.

I looked over to Ant and before I could say anything, he finally spoke. "I understand, bruh. You know it's nothing but love on this end. Gone home to your wifey and let us clean this shit up."

"That's love, fam," I replied while chucking the deuces and leaving the warehouse.

Before pulling out of the parking lot, I sat there in the driver's seat of my car thinking about this being my last run in the streets. It was kind of a bittersweet moment, but I was sure that being able to spend more time with Sky and building our future together would be more of a reward in the long run.

I put my car in drive and turned on the radio. "How befitting," I thought to myself because Tupac's "Hail Mary" was on the radio.

I ain't a killer, but don't push me
Revenge is like the sweetest joy next to getting pussy

I smiled to myself in agreement as I pulled out of the parking lot and headed home to be with my queen.

Chapter Six

Sky

Over the next couple of months, I made sure to wear loose fitting clothing and nothing that would restrict my now slightly protruding belly. I wasn't big enough for anyone to notice that I was pregnant, but I was damn sure noticing the change myself.

I tried my best to keep a low profile by staying in the house for the most part. The furthest I went these days was around the corner to Rayne's whenever Aston wasn't home, to my doctor's appointments and back. I still visited Julius', but mostly during the day when I knew that he'd be out handling his business; and I would only stay long enough to cook so that he'd have a home cooked meal once he made it in from a long day's work.

I did my best to avoid both JuJu and Aston at all costs, which gave me more time to spend with Raye and make up for lost time.

Luckily for me, JuJu was really understanding about me spending so much time with Raye. I'd told him that we were patching up our friendship. Normally, he would have wanted me to be all up under him, but I think that he was silently thanking GOD that Raye and I had reconciled our differences and were now back on speaking terms because he had been so preoccupied with his "business" as he calls it, that he really hadn't had much time to spend with me lately anyway.

As for me, I was just glad for the temporary distraction. It kept me from having to make up and keep up with so many lies.

I had been staying back at Nana's for the most part, and I knew that she was starting to get suspicious because she had started making little comments about my clothes fitting me so loosely. She'd even made mention about me sleeping so much; but she still hadn't made her way around to asking, and damn it, I wasn't volunteering the information. My lips were sealed! I still hadn't let my secret out of the bag to anyone other than Raye and, of course, Aston.

"Damn...Aston," I thought aloud as my thoughts started to get away from me and I allowed a tear to fall while getting in my feelings because the thought of him made my heart ache. I wished that things had been different between us.

I'd managed to keep my secret under wraps for the time being, but I wasn't sure how much longer this would last. I mean, hell, it wasn't like time was rewinding itself. If anything, it was speeding up.

My phone rang, bringing me back to the present as I stood in the bathroom mirror at Nana's with my shirt lifted, looking at my baby bump.

I looked down at the phone ringing and vibrating on the bathroom counter and immediately felt another sting to my heart. I almost started not to answer, but knowing that I couldn't hide out forever, I answered in the most chipper voice that I could muster up because the last thing that I wanted to do was alert Julius of how I was feeling.

"Hey, handsome," I cooed into the phone.

"What's up, my queen?"

"Not much, just lying across the bed," I said, telling a little white lie as I made my way back to my room and sat down on the edge of the bed.

"Well, check it. I know ah nigga been tied up lately, and I'm sorry if I haven't been making time for you like I should. I wanna make it up you... Starting tonight."

"Awww, bae, it's okay. You don't have to explain anything to me. I know that my man is a boss," I said, laying it on thick, "and when duty calls, I also know that you have to answer," I said sweetly.

He chuckled into the phone before replying. "Sky," he called into the phone.

"Yeah?"

"I love the hell outta yo ass."

I was now grinning from ear to ear as I replied, "I love you too, bae."

"Yeah…you betta," he joked. "You missing your man yet?"

"Always," I replied quickly.

"Good, I was hoping that you would say that."

"And why is that?" I flirted into the phone.

"Because I'm pulling up in your Nana's driveway. Ah nigga been missing yo' lil sexy ass. Come outside. I'm about to kidnap my queen and take her back to the palace where she belongs." I could hear the smile in his voice as he made that statement before hanging up in my ear.

I immediately started to panic. There would be no way in hell I'd be able to hide this shit from him any longer, I could just feel it in my bones. I wanted to grab an overnight bad and throw as many big shirts into it as I could find but I knew that I'd look suspect, especially since I'd practically moved in with him over the last few months and most of my things were already over there. He'd definitely want to know what the hell I'm doing with a big ass duffle bag and I was positive that my cover would be blown at that point.

It was like an unspoken rule for Julius and I to walk around the house either naked or half-naked, so I didn't know how in the hell I was gonna pull this one off, but I was gonna have to put on my big girl drawls and make it do what it do.

My mind immediately went into survival mode as the wheels in my head started turning. I grabbed my purse and keys, trying to figure out how in the hell I'd be able to keep this secret, while making my way out of the door.

~~~

As we sat on the couch watching a rerun that I'd wanted to catch up on of *Love & Hip Hop Atlanta*, I could barely concentrate as I sat between Julius's strong legs while he proceeded to give me one of the best back rubs that I'd ever had. It felt so good and I wanted to relish the moment, despite listening to the little voice in my head that continuously reminded me that his back rubs were usually followed by some real life happy endings.

But maybe this is what we both needed. He and I hadn't had a real live love making session in almost a whole month so we were both overdue. I was yearning to feel my man, and apparently, he was feeling the same because he soon started to place tiny wet kisses all over the back of my neck. His touch was electric and I could feel the hairs on the back of my neck stand up. I quivered with anticipation as I threw my head back and enjoyed this moment.

His hands were like feathers as they traced up and down my arms, lighting a new fire in me that I had no idea something so small would ignite. This was it. I could no longer sit through this torture. "I'll just roll with the punches and deal with the consequences," I thought to myself as I stood from the couch, turned around and straddled him. Just as quick, I threw my arms around his neck and kissed him with everything in me.

I needed him to feel what I was feeling at that very moment. I needed him to want me just as much as I wanted him. When I felt his tongue entwined with mine, I knew then that we were about to make magic together.

He took his time lifting my sweater, breaking the kiss long enough to get it over my head, and starting back to the task at hand. He then reached behind me and unsnapped my bra without a hiccup, releasing my already erect nipples and he wasted no time lifting them both to meet his wet mouth at the same time.

We were both so caught up in the moment that I don't think he ever even noticed my small little tummy, as he took his time pleasing me while I continued to hold on to his shoulders and grind myself onto him.

Without warning, he stood to his feet, lifting me in the process, and walked over to the wall next to the fireplace while palming my ass to help keep me up.

My breathing was out of control as I braced myself for what was about to come. Julius quickly hoisted me up against the wall and flashed that sexy, dimpled smile that I fell in love with from the very beginning. For a moment, we'd gotten lost in one another's eyes. I was in a daze gazing into his deep browns, until he slid my panties to the side and slid into my opening.

I don't know when he was able to take his pants off, but when I looked down, his pants were dangling around his ankles and the muscles in his thighs were flexing as he rocked in and out of my honey pot. Looking down and seeing my juices glistening on his thick rod as he moved meticulously in and out of special place gave me a rush.

Before long, I'd started rolling my hips and riding him like a rancher as he dipped down and thrust upward as far as he could go. It was a pleasurable hurt and each time he hit my g-spot, I would call out to GOD himself. This nigga was skilled as hell when it came to pleasing me, and if I didn't appreciate shit else he did for me, I appreciated how he took control and handled his own behind closed doors.

When I felt him open my cheeks wider and plunge deeper, my eyes bucked like saucers from the impact and I couldn't help but call out in painful bliss. "Ohhhhh GOD…Julius," I panted. "Yesssss."

He didn't say a word but he buried his head into the crook of my neck and grunted as he moved strategically in and out of my tunnel of love. I'd erupted more times than I could count and I was out of breath and drained to the max, but it seemed as if Julius was just getting started so I tightened my legs around his waist, rolled my hips and rocked out with my man.

"Damn, bae... You feel so good," he said breathlessly into my neck.

I was stuck between a subsiding orgasm and the rise of another one so my words were paralyzed and all I could do was moan as he continued to stir my honey pot until he couldn't hold it anymore and exploded inside of me. We were so spent that neither of us could move so instead of him immediately putting me down, he and I just used one another to continue to hold ourselves up as we struggled happily to catch our breaths.

When he finally let me down, my legs were like string cheese as I collapsed, almost busting my ass, but he was there to catch my fall. About all he could do was catch my fall because we never made it any further than the floor right in from of the wall next to the fireplace; thankful that it wasn't on because I was hot as hell as we both laid on the plush rug, falling into slumbers of our own and sleeping like babies.

L., NISHA

Chapter Seven

Sky

I woke up and jetted to the downstairs bathroom so quick that you would have thought that I had hot coals in my ass. When I made it to the bathroom, I immediately fell to my knees as vomit spewed from my mouth. I didn't have anything on my stomach but that didn't stop my body from puking its brains out. The only thing that would come up was a yellow, acid-tasting liquid that let me know that my stomach was on E. I was gagging something terrible and felt like I would cough up a lung at any moment.

My mouth was open and my tongue was hanging out as I damn near choked to death while tears formed in the corners of my eyes. I was so out of it that I hadn't even noticed that Julius had come in. I guess I'd woke him up with all of the noise.

"Ohhhh, shit!" he yelled as he moved quickly to my side, patting my back with one hand, and holding my hair back with the other. "Bae, you straight?" he asked, looking down on me to make sure that I was gonna be okay.

I was out of breath and I could only shake my head to let him know that I was fine.

Once the freak show was over, he told me to go lay down, but I already knew what was wrong with me so there was no use. This little bundle was already making his or her mark in the world, letting me know that he or she would not take any shit. I had slept through dinner and would have already had more than a couple of snacks by now and I guess the baby was letting me know that this shit wasn't gonna fly. So instead of going to lay down like Julius had already advised me to do, I figured I'd just make my way into the kitchen while he stayed behind to clean my mess.

My back was hurting, my stomach was in knots, and my throat was dry as the Sahara Desert. I looked down at my bare feet on the tile and even noticed that they were a little more swollen than normal.

"Ugghhh, the doctor said that this would happen," I mumbled while rolling my eyes and opening the refrigerator to grab the lunch meat, mayo and cheese so that I could make me a quick sandwich.

"The doctor said what would happen?" Julius asked, making his presence known as he leaned against the countertop with his arms folded, eyeing me like he could see straight through me.

I slowly turned around, trying to give myself time to come up with a quick and believable lie, but when I saw the look on his face, I just broke down in tears. Once again these damn pregnancy hormones had made my emotions betray me as the flood gates were opened and tears poured freely from my eyes.

Through blurred vision, I could see the seriousness in Julius' face turn to a look of concern as he lunged towards me and cradled me in his arms, allowing me to cry my eyes out. It was sort of therapeutic, and with him here by my side, I felt like a weight had been lifted off of my shoulders, and that I could conquer the world.

I guessed I would just have to woman up and let him know what the hell is going on. Now don't get too excited, though. I mean, hell, just because I have to let him know about the baby, doesn't mean that I'm stupid enough to mention anything about the paternity of the child. But the way I see it is that I have a man that loves me to death and wants to be with me, and if he loves me, I know that he'll love our creation as well because I don't have the time or energy these days to be chasing Aston's ass down about a baby that may not even be his. Besides, he's made it perfectly clear that he wants no parts of me or this baby.

Through sniffles, I dried my eyes and managed to look up and when our eyes met, the love in his eyes reassured me that I was making the right decision by telling him. His eyes also let me know that all that I'd needed this entire time was right here in front of me.

"Julius, we need to talk," I said, taking his hand, pulling him into the dining room and pulling out a chair for him to sit down in.

"So wassup, bae?" he asked seriously.

And just like that, once again, I had completely lost my nerve and was no longer the confident young woman that I was less than a minute ago. Wanting to hurry and get this over with, I blurted out the first this that came to mind.

"Julius…I'm pregnant!"

Silence.

"Did you hear me?" I asked, just above a whisper with my head now hung low.

"Yea…I did," he said, getting up from his chair and coming to stand directly in from of the chair that I was sitting in, right across from the chair that I'd pulled out for him to sit in.

I couldn't hold my tongue any longer and I let the word vomit that was threatening to erupt, take over. "Well, say something, damn it!" I yelled as he just stood there looking down at me.

"How far are you?" he asked sternly.

"A little over five months," I mumbled.

I could see him mentally calculating the time frames in his head before finally exhaling and grabbing my arms to pull me into his chest.

"Why are you just now saying something, Sky?"

"Because I know that you didn't want any kids right now and I just couldn't take being rejected again," I said, slipping up before I was able to catch myself.

He placed his hands on my shoulders and pushed me back lightly so that he could look into my eyes. "What do you mean, rejected again?" he asked with his eyebrows raised. "When have I ever rejected you?"

Silence.

"That's what I thought."

"I didn't mean it like that. I just...I was–"

"You were what?" he yelled, cutting me off mid-sentence before continuing. "Look, Sky, I'm gonna say this and be done with this because this is about to give ah nigga a headache just that quick. No, I didn't want any kids right away because I wanted to do shit the right way with you. I wanted to make you my wife first, but GOD saw fit to bless us with a child and I'm thankful for that. For me, it's like I'm getting a second chance at life through you and this baby; so of course I'm gonna do what I need to do and step up to the plate. But what I won't tolerate is disrespect. I didn't miss the little comment that you just made, and just in case yo' ass," he said, pushing me in the forehead with his index finger, "didn't get the memo, I'm not a dumb ass nigga and I damn sholl ain't no sucker! So if you fucking me over, Sky, we gonna have some real life issues."

"Julius, what in the hell are you trying to say?" I asked, yelling with tears and snot flying all over the place.

He grabbed my chin in between his index finger and thumb as he guided my face towards his. I thought that he was about to kiss me, but when I felt a pain shooting through my bottom lip, it was then that I realized that this muthafucka had bit me.

I yelled out in pain. "Ahhhhhhhh, shit!" My normal reaction was to slap the shit out of him but he caught my hand before I could land the hit.

Looking directly into his eyes, I didn't even recognize the person that was staring back at me. This nigga had gone from zero to a hundred real quick.

He then closed the gap in between us and through clenched teeth, he spoke. "I don't know what the hell is up with you, but when you love someone, you don't keep secrets like this. This was supposed to be a happy time for us and you done fucked it up. Now go get dressed so I can take your ass home because I just can't bring myself to believe that not only have you stood here in my face and disrespected me, but you don't know me well enough to know that you could have come to and talked to me about anything.

"I'd have to be a real asshole, to believe that you didn't think that I would be there for yo' ass throughout this pregnancy. That's some bullshit and you know it!"

I just stood there taking in his every word and trying to decide if I should chime in now or later because this nigga was clearly a damn schizo.

"How's that bullshit, Julius?" I asked.

"Mannn, let's just back up, take a few days away from one another and re-evaluate our relationship because clearly something is wrong if you feel like you gotta be keeping secrets and shit and can't talk to yo man... Somebody that you claim to be so damn in love with!"

I was at a loss for words, but what in the hell could I say because I had just got served. I turned hard on the balls of my feet and stomped away, and making sure that I was out of his reach before yelling, "Love isn't supposed hurt!"

Hell, what else could I say? I was pregnant and in my feelings but he had every right to feel like he felt. I mean, I would never tell him that, but it is what it is.

"I couldn't agree with you more," he said sadly.

I stopped in my tracks. "Are you trying to tell me something?"

"I'm hurting and you haven't even taken the time to even act like you care. In so many words, I'm telling you that I love you and that I'm rocking with you. I just want you to keep shit a hunnit with me. Respect me like I respect you!" he raised his voice. "You round here hiding pregnancies and shit, lying and holding out like this ain't ah nigga baby or something. Hell, should I be worried right now, Sky?"

"Are you insinuating that I'm a whore?"

"Hell nah! But what I am insinuating is that yo' ass on some other shit right now!"

Silence.

"Figures… Now you just wanna stand there looking crazy but that's because you know something ain't right. I've known you long enough to know that you wouldn't have a problem with putting me in my place if you felt that I was saying something wrong; but you haven't had shit of value to say since I started talking….and you're right, love isn't supposed to hurt so maybe you don't love me like you think you do," he said, putting way too much emphasis on the word think.

For once in my life, I didn't have a comeback because I knew in my heart of hearts that he was right. My ass is living foul and I guess he could sense that, but instead of hanging my ass out on a limb, he was actually trying to do the right thing.

I sluggishly made my way up the stairs to the bedroom in deep thought. I gotta make this shit right. I can't leave any stones unturned with him. I love this man, and it's clear that all he wants to do is love me, too, or does he?

Chapter Eight

Julius

I drove through the city, making a few pit stops to check on a few business investments, but I couldn't help but to think about Sky in the process. After our lil spat a few weeks ago, I had been giving her ass the cold shoulder so it made me happy to know that she was actually still showing some type of interest in ah nigga.

Sky had been calling me for about two weeks straight, leaving messages on my voicemail, texting me constantly, and even going as far as doing pop-up visits, hoping to catch me at home, I guess.

I could always tell when she'd been there because even though I had been keeping my distance from her, she still made sure that I was taken care of. She still came over to clean and do my laundry during the week, she would always cook to make sure that I would have something to eat when I got home, and the dead giveaway was that the house would always smell of her favorite perfume, Chance by Chanel.

Some may think that I was being petty, but I'd like to think that I was just protecting my heart. When I first got with Sky, she was fresh out of a relationship and I know that sometimes when you've been dealing with someone for so long, even when it's over, it's not really over, if ya know what I mean. That's why when she mentioned that she was pregnant, it kind of threw me for a loop. The first thing I wanted to know after finding out how far along she was, is one, why in the hell did she wait so long to tell me if she knew that I was the baby's father and two, if there a possibility that this could be dude's baby?

I didn't want shit to come off like I didn't trust her, but that little comment she'd made still had me feeling some type of way. It had damn sho' shifted the momentum that night, and lately, it's been on my mind real heavy. I'd even reached out to Peanut and asked him to put his ears and eyes to the street to see if she was still dealing with dude.

Now according to my calculations and how far she says that she is, I knew that the baby should be mine, and based on that, I was gonna do what I have to do to be there for the both of them. At least until I had proof telling me otherwise; because like I said, you can never be too sure. But in an effort to get back on track, I was just gonna call her later on. You know, see where we were gonna go from here, because ah nigga can't even front, I been missing her like crazy, and the fact that she hadn't given up made me want her around that much more.

~~~

I pulled up in Raye's driveway and was glad to see that Aston's car wasn't there. Normally I would have called first to be sure that he wasn't home, but it had completely slipped my mind with all that I had going on lately, and I needed to speak with my bestie ASAP. I needed her advice in the worst way.

My emotions were a wreck and I couldn't help but to be in my feelings about the way that Julius was treating me. I'd been crying non-stop ever since the night of our little fight and I didn't know if I was coming or going anymore.

I stood on the porch ringing the doorbell like a mad woman. I could hear footsteps approaching the door and yelling from the other side.

"Who the hell is it, ringing my damn doorbell like they crazy this early in the damn morning?"

The only problem was that whereas normally it would be Rayne talking shit to me for ringing the doorbell like I was crazy, it wasn't her voice at all that I was hearing.

I immediately tensed up as the door flew open and there he stood, looking good enough to eat. Even when he'd just hopped up out of his sleep half-naked, he was still handsome.

We stood there staring at one another for what seemed like hours; me admiring his beautifully sculpted chest and humongous print in his boxers, and him zoning in on my now extremely noticeable baby bump. When I noticed him giving me the once over, I became self-conscious. I started fidgeting, wishing that my shorts were a little bit longer, and pulling on my cami to make sure that my belly was covered. I even noticed myself running my fingers through my uncombed hair, trying to smooth it down some.

"Damn you for not getting dressed and combing yo' hair this morning. I bet from now on, you'll think twice before just rolling out of bed, brushing your teeth and hopping in the car," I thought as I silently scolded myself in my head.

Seeing as how he wasn't going to say anything to me, I figured that I'd just go ahead and break the ice. "I'm sorry, I didn't see your car out front...I mean if I would have known...umm...never mind...is ummm...is Raye here?" I asked, stumbling over my words a lot more than I would've liked to.

Without making eye contact or speaking to me, he sighed and pushed the door open, leaving me standing there, and looking stupid, to let myself in. I stepped into the house, pulling the door closed and locking it behind me, just in time enough to hear Aston's room door slam.

I proceeded to walk down the hall to Raye's room, bypassing my old room as well as Aston's current one. It seemed as if the hall had been stretched to infinity and beyond because that was the longest walk ever. I felt like a jump off tipping out of the hotel room at four in the morning, trying to make sure no one saw me.

When I made it to Raye's door, I knocked softly before letting myself in. I knew that she was a light sleeper and that she would hear me. I pushed the door open and let myself into the room, and just as I'd suspected, she was already sitting up in the bed, with a unit on her face.

When she saw me come through the door, she smiled. "What are you doing out this early?" she quizzed.

"Sorry to wake you, I just needed to talk," I said, sniffling and trying to stop the waterworks that I felt stirring up.

She adjusted the covers and straightened her posture. "Oh no, it's okay. Besides, it was my big head ass brother that woke me when he slammed that door," she said, smiling. "Now lay on back and tell me what's wrong," she said playfully as she picked up and notepad and pen from her nightstand.

I laughed a little at her attempt to lighten the mood. "You playing, but hell, I may need a psychiatrist for real, Raye. Shit is all fucked up and I just don't know how much more I can take."

"Let me guess. You told JuJu that you're pregnant?" she inquired.

"Yea...I did," I replied, dropping my head and letting a silent tear fall as I continued to reveal all of the details of what had transpired between JuJu and I; not stopping short of the callous but brief encounter that I'd just had with Aston.

When I finished purging, I felt like a new person. With Raye, I spared no details and left no questions unanswered. "This is definitely my girl," I thought to myself as my mind started to drift off in space, wondering how in the hell I'd let things get to the point that it had with the two of us. Nevertheless, I was glad that we were back on track now.

Aston

Damn, I hadn't expected to see Sky today, and out of all places, here at the house. We'd been doing pretty well lately when it came to avoiding one another, so I gotta admit that ah nigga was definitely caught off guard and thrown for a loop when I opened the door and she was standing there, looking like she hadn't had a decent sleep in months. She still had on her night clothes and her hair was standing every which way on top of her head, and even with her not being dressed to a tee or her hair being laid as it normally would've been, she was still the most beautiful woman that I'd ever laid eyes on.

When my eyes traveled downward and landed on her belly, my heart fluttered and my stomach did a couple of flips at the thought of her carrying my seed. I wanted to reach out and grab her, stroke her hair and stare into her eyes, while telling her how much I loved her and how I'd missed her, but my pride just wouldn't let me do it. Instead, I opted to continue as if she meant absolutely nothing to me.

I could tell that she was hurt. I could see the pain in her eyes and the worry etched in her forehead, but I didn't care because in that moment, all I wanted was to make her hurt like she'd done me. Hell, I'm human, but my pride had been shot to hell, so yea, I felt that I still had to play the part. At least that's how I felt before I'd made my way back here to the room. Now I was sitting here thinking about how creep I was gonna be if the baby that she was carrying turned out to be mine. Shit, I wouldn't want my seed to come into the world and I miss his or her debut.

"Fuck!" I mumbled to myself. "This shit is so fucked up, it's unbelievable."

I heard Raye's room door open in the distance and I could hear them saying their good-byes and Sky telling her that she would keep her posted about something.

"Now is my chance," I thought to myself. It was time for me to get my shit together, especially if I was about to be someone's daddy, and what better place to start than with Sky? So I got up from the bed and made my way to the door.

When I opened my room door, Sky immediately dropped her head and sped up her walk, trying to avoid making any kind of eye contact with me, and had this been a few minutes prior, I would have let her ass keep it moving, but because I was tryna man up, that shit ain't acceptable.

"Yo, Sky," my voice boomed as I called out to her.

She stopped dead in her tracks. She just stood there without turning to face me. She didn't move another muscle; it was like she was frozen in time. She didn't look back, she didn't turn around, she damn sholl didn't answer me and if I hadn't known any better, I would have thought that she had just stopped breathing altogether. After what seemed like hours of her standing there with her back to me, and me waiting for her to answer, I realized that it just wasn't happening, so I went ahead and took the first step, just as she'd done when I came to the door this morning.

"Can I holla at cha for a second?"

"Oh, so now you wanna talk?"

Silence.

"When I wanted to talk, you–"

I could see where this shit was about to go and I refused to let things get off course. So before she could say another mumbling word, I cut her off. "Look, I know you're pissed off right now, but we not about to do the going back and forth shit. I didn't stop you for that. I'm gonna own up to my shit, you're gonna own up to yours. We're gonna discuss this shit like adults and try our best to get along and do what's best for everyone involved," I said with finality in my voice as I turned and walked back into the room, plopping down on my bed and waiting for her to come in and do the same.

When I realized that she still hadn't made her way into the room, I sighed and called out to her. "Yo, Sky, right now ain't the time for you to be in your feelings. We got some shit that we need to discuss and I can't do that without your cooperation, so bring ya ass in here, nah!"

She was really starting to piss me the hell off and I was about two seconds short of cursing her ass out and sending her on her way. The fact was, I knew that I was still in love with this girl and of course, I hated to see her hurt, but in this particular circumstance, I had to put my feelings on the backburner and so should she. That's the only way that we were gonna be able to focus on the right now; and whether or not either of us likes it, the baby that she is carrying was definitely the first on the "right now" list.

She slowly made her way into the room and stood next to the door with her arms folded over her belly as if she was protecting the baby from the conversation that we were about to have.

"Come on, man. Sit down and stop being dramatic," I demanded while trying to keep myself from getting aggravated.

She reluctantly took a seat on the edge of the bed and, just as she did in the hallway, she waited patiently for me to kick the conversation off, and that was A-Okay with me. I just wanted to hurry and get this shit done and over with!

"Listen, Sky. I don't wanna argue with you, I just wanna know how sure you are that the baby that you're carrying is mine?" I asked, looking into her eyes, searching for an answer. In my heart I already knew what was up but I just couldn't believe that my baby girl had done ah nigga this dirty, even with the proof sitting right here in my face.

"Aston, I never meant to hurt you, but–"

I had to cut her off mid-sentence. "Sky, just answer the question, ma. All of that extra shit ain't even necessary because what's already done is done," I said, meaning every word.

She shook her head up and down in agreement before speaking. "Well, for what it's worth, I'm still sorry," she said with glossy eyes. "I just wanna come clean. Shit, I'm done with all of the lying and sneaking around. This shit is for the birds. I never wanted to be 'that girl,' you know, the one to get caught up in this ole *Jerry Springer* shit; but I'd be lying if I told you that I'm one thousand percent sure that the baby that I'm carrying is yours. But there's definitely a fifty percent chance of you being the father," she spoke softly as tears cascaded down her beautiful face.

Looking into her face, I could tell that she'd had many of these crying sessions and it pained me to know that I hadn't been there for her like I'd always promised her that I would. In hindsight, it was like I'd fucked her over all over again… Inadvertently? Definitely, but I'd fucked her over nonetheless.

I guess this was her get back and I knew in my heart that she was dead ass wrong for handling me the way that she had, yet I still wanted to love her. I still wanted to be there for her and this baby. I wanted to protect her from all of the shit and people that I should have protected her from in the very beginning. I wanted to be her knight in shining armor again.

"I guess I have no choice but to respect that since you're being truthful, huh?" I said as a statement more than a question, and not waiting for her to answer before continuing.

"I know what I said when you first told me that you were pregnant, and that was out of hurt and anger for the most part; and just being honest, I had been doing really well with sticking to that up until I seen you today. While you were in there with Raye, I got to thinking and I really don't want to miss out on anything else in this baby's life. I mean, hell, what if this is my baby? I don't want to just sit back and watch while another nigga is doing what I should have been doing all along." I paused for effect as I looked into her eyes to see her soul smile. She looked as if she could finally breathe again. "I wanna go with you to your doctor appointments, I wanna be around to feel his or her kick for the first time, and I damn sholl wanna be there for the birth. Mine or not, I don't wanna take any more chances missing out on life's little miracles."

"Aston, I really appreciate that and I am so sorry for everything," she said again before throwing her arms around my neck and hugging me for dear life.

We sat and talked for a few hours after that and it was just like old times... Well, the times before we were a couple anyway, but that was okay with me. We talked about the progress of the baby, how she'd been feeling and we'd even made plans to start shopping for all of the necessities that the baby would need once it got here.

I was really enjoying the new us. I felt refreshed because I had my friend back and, according to her, she was just happy that I was finally speaking to her again. Although I wasn't too thrilled about it, she was even open and honest with me about the nigga JuJu and their relationship status. I was understanding for the most part, but I'd be damned if I missed anymore doctor appointments and I was sure to explain that to her.

She claimed that it shouldn't be a problem because he hadn't made it to any appointments thus far. She said that he'd been really busy lately and hadn't had the time like he used to have. Sounded like a fuck nigga to me, but that wasn't my business, though. As long as neither of their asses came with any bullshit about my seed, everything would be all good.

Before she left, we made plans to talk later on. We needed that little talk and I was glad that I had finally manned up and made it happen.

I got up to get dressed and hit the streets. With a baby on the way, I had to make sure that my money stayed plentiful and I couldn't do that by being cooped up in the house all day. I needed to be out making moves.

Sky and I were back on speaking terms, I had finally acknowledged the possibility of me having a baby on the way and I had all intentions of making sure that the three of us wanted for nothing.

Chapter Nine

Sky

A month had gone by and it was time for my routine doctor's visit. Julius and I had made up some time ago and he'd promised to start being more active, yet there he was again...nowhere to be found.

He was supposed to be back to the house by eight thirty to pick me up because from his house, the ride to the doctor's office was about forty-five minutes to an hour, depending on traffic. Here it was eight fifty and I hadn't heard so much as a peep from him since this time yesterday morning; and even then that was only via text.

I had even called his phone a few times but was sent straight to voicemail. This definitely wasn't like him, but then again, nothing was like him these days, and things were rarely ever what they seemed anymore. Ever since I'd told Julius about me being pregnant, things had changed between us. I mean, granted, I was still staying with him and he was still taking care of me, but I realized now that I was pretty much going through this pregnancy alone, with the exception of Aston checking in on me every day.

He had definitely stepped up to the plate in that regard. He called me constantly to check on me and the baby, just to make sure that we didn't need anything. According to Raye, Aston had been in the streets non-stop since our little talk. She said that he'd even gone out on his own and started buying stuff here and there that he thought the baby would need.

I heaved a deep breath before picking up my phone to make one last call on my way out of the door. I refused to go to another doctor's appointment alone, and although I'd withheld the information about my doctor's appointment from Aston because I'd figured that JuJu would finally make some time for me and want to go, I'm sure that he wouldn't mind the last minute call anyway.

"Wassup, baby girl?" he answered groggily into the phone.

"Well, good morning, sleepy head. I was wondering if you would like to meet at the doctor's office today."

"What? Today?" he asked frantically. "It's not time yet, is it?"

"No, crazy!" I exclaimed, laughing at how foolish he sounded. "I'm only a little over six months pregnant.

I'm just going for a regular checkup," I said as I walked out of the door, closing and locking it behind me and making my way to my car.

"What time is your appointment?"

"Ten," I replied barley above a whisper.

I could hear him fumbling around on the other end of the phone while I waited patiently for an answer.

"TEN?" he yelled into the phone.

"I know its last minute, so if you can't make it, that's fine, Aston. It's not a big deal," I spoke apologetically into the phone.

"Mannnn, shut up wit' yo big head ass," he replied, laughing a little before he continued. "I'm getting up now. Text me the directions," he said, hanging up in my ear.

I started the ignition and text him the directions as requested before pulling out of the long driveway and making my way to the doctor's office.

~~~

Luckily for Aston, he had a much shorter ride to the doctor's office than me and we ended up pulling in at the same exact time. As I gathered my keys and purse, preparing to exit the car, Aston had already made his way over to the driver's side of my car, opening the door to help me out.

"Wassup, ma?" he asked as he helped me out of the car and enveloped me in a much needed hug.

I hugged him back, getting lightheaded as he intoxicated me with his signature Gucci Guilty cologne. As we made our way to the entrance and he held the door open for me, I couldn't help but to sneak a peek at him on the low. I didn't miss a beat as I admired how good he looked even when he was dressed down. He had on a pair of gray sweatpants; with a crisp white V-neck t-shirt, and a fresh pair of gray and white Js. "The nigga is still as fine as the first day that I'd ever laid eyes on him, which was only part of the reason why I fell so deep in love with him from the jump," I thought to myself.

I passed the threshold and made my way straight to the counter where the receptionist sat, so that I could check in. Once I'd signed myself in, Aston and I made our way over to a pair of vacant seats and waited for our turn to be called while making light conversation about nothing in particular.

After several minutes, I heard the nurse call my name. "Ms. Banks." Without answering, Aston and I both stood and made our way over to the nurse. We followed her down the hall as she verified my contact information while in stride.

"Skyla, please have a seat on the table for me," she said as she took out all of the necessities to take my vitals. "You can have a seat right over there, sir," she said, speaking to Aston and pointing to the chair located directly in front of the examination table.

After an array of questions about how I'd been feeling these days and giving her the run down on any changes that I'd noticed with my body since my last checkup, she recorded the information that I'd given her and proceeded to take and document my vitals. Once she finished, she handed me a cup and a cover-up, and instructed me to leave a urine sample in the restroom behind the mirror and to disrobe from the waist down once I was back in the room.

I did as I was told and after a few more minutes, Dr. Nassir made his way into the room.

"Ms. Banks, we meet again," he said in an upbeat tone, "and I see that you've brought us some company today," he said, walking over to Aston to introduce himself. "You must be the proud father," he asked, extending his hand to shake Aston's.

"Ummm...actually, Dr. Nassir," I said getting ready to answer his question about Aston being the father of my child when Aston butted in, extending his hand to shake Dr. Nassir's.

"I sure am, sir. My name is Aston. Nice to meet you," he said with a wide smile, and a wink in my direction.

"Very well, Aston. Nice to meet you. I'm Dr. Nassir, the proud physician," he said jokingly.

My heart melted on the spot and I was now grinning from ear to ear. It felt good to be accepted by Aston and even better to hear him acknowledge my child as his own and not as a possible like a game of Spades. It made me respect him that much more.

After washing his hands, Dr. Nassir got started on my exam. He turned the monitor on and after identifying all of the baby's body parts, he asked with a smile, "So...Ms.

Banks, do you still not want to know the sex of your baby?"

Simultaneously Aston and I both spoke up, me saying "no" and him replying "yes."

I let out a nervous chuckle while looking at Dr. Nassir, feeling slightly embarrassed.

"I guess we didn't get a chance to discuss this little detail before arrival," I said, eyeing Aston.

"Sky, why don't you wanna know what we're having?"

"Aston, I really just wanted it to be a surprise. I mean, as long as the baby is healthy, that's all that should matter…right?" I asked, hoping that he'd see things my way.

"Nah, ma. Ah nigga can't get jiggy wit' dat shit. I need to know what we're having, baby girl."

I looked at him looking back at me, and I could actually see the seriousness in his eyes. It was like he was yearning to know what it was that we were having.

"Maybe I should give you two a minute," Dr. Nassir interjected.

"No... It's fine, doc. You don't have to leave. You can let us know what we are having."

He nodded his head and smiled as he excused himself. "I'm going to send Eva in. She's our x-ray technician and she will be able to perform a transvaginal exam on you so that you two can both see your baby in living color, up close and personal in 4D," he said with a smile while adjusting his glasses before continuing. "She will also be able to confirm for you what you're going to be having as well," he said before making his way out of the door.

When I looked over to see Aston grinning like a Cheshire cat, I knew then that I was making the right decision, and he actually looked rather excited about the whole ordeal.

As for me, I was just happy to be getting a smidge of attention from at least one of the men that I just so happened to be in love with. I laid back and relaxed on the table while waiting for Eva to come in. The examination lasted about twenty-five minutes, tops, and we were out of there in no time.

When we made it outside of the doctor's office, we agreed to meet back at his place and take his car to the mall to do a little shopping for our new addition.

~~~

As we walked through the store laughing and talking, I couldn't have been happier to have found out what I was having, and, more importantly, to be able to share the entire experience with Aston. We walked through the entire mall, from the top to the bottom, going in and out of every children's store that we could find. We bought up all of the cutest and latest baby fashions.

I was surprisingly having the time of my life, which was odd because normally if I wasn't shopping for myself, I didn't even like to step foot inside of a mall. I guess I was growing up after all.

When I snapped out of my thought and looked to my right, I notices Aston smiling at me and I couldn't help but to smile right back.

"What in the heck are you cheesing so hard about?" I asked.

"You know my lil dude is gonna be a junior, right?" he stated more than asked as he stopped me in my tracks by placing his hand on my belly.

It was like he and the baby had an instant connection because as soon as Aston placed his hands on my stomach, the baby started kicking.

"See! He likes that idea, too," he said jokingly.

"Yea, yea, yea," I replied, smiling as Aston reached up without any warning and moved my hair from my face.

"Baby girl, you know you're still as beautiful as ever to me," he said while caressing my cheek.

I couldn't answer him. He'd caught me completely off guard and I was now blushing from ear to ear.

"You don't have to say anything right now because I know that you still have that whole other situation that you are dealing with right now, but I want us to try again, Sky. Baby girl, I been missing you like crazy."

My heart was actually skipping beats and it seemed as if I couldn't process what he was saying fast enough. Before I knew it, he'd drawn me in and we'd locked lips right in front of Baby Gap and Express for the entire mall to see. I guess we didn't have any shame in our game.

Chapter Ten

Julius

I had no particular destination in mind, but I knew that I wasn't ready to go home just yet. I'd dived head first back into the game after Sky dropped the news on me about her being pregnant. I'm not sure why, but for some reason, I felt complete when I was out here getting my hands dirty, so despite me promising to go legit and spend more time with her, I'd been doing just the opposite.

Sky and I hadn't been vibing like we used to and I couldn't put my finger on why that was, but I could probably bet my last dollar that I had a good idea of what was wrong.

I don't feel in my spirit that the baby is mine, and I know what everybody is thinking. They're probably selling out talking about how much of a no good ass nigga I was for acting like that but hell, I just wasn't convinced.

The connection that I'd once had with her seemed to be dwindling, and I could honestly say that in my heart of hearts, I knew for a fact that she hadn't been a hunnit with me.

Hell, look at how long her ass waited to tell ah nigga that she was pregnant. Any other chick would have been too excited to keep something like that in, especially with it being our first child together. Not to mention the little comment that she had slipped and made. I may have let that shit fly for the time being, but I definitely had my ears to the street.

I had been the perfect nigga to her ass so there would have been no reason for me to believe that she honestly thought that she couldn't come to me and tell me that she was pregnant and expect me not do what I needed to do to be there and provide for her and the child. To be honest, I was kind of hurt because she played me like I was some ole bum ass nigga.

Yea, I was definitely in my feelings as I made my rounds to pick up my money, all with Skyla intruding on my thoughts. Just as I turned into the projects, my phone rang, snapping me out of my pity party.

"Wassup, brutha?" I answered into the phone after seeing Skeet's name on my caller ID.

"Yo chick is wassup."

At this point, I was sitting straight up in my seat and my ears had tuned in like satellite dishes.

"Fuck you mean, bruh?"

"Sheeiittt, bruh, I hate to be a bearer of bad news, but me and Ant just left the mall and we saw her ass all hugged up on some lil nigga in the middle of the mall."

I had to give myself a chance to process the information that he was laying on me before speaking. My blood was boiling at how fucking disrespectful Sky had gotten in such a short amount of time.

"My nigga, are you sure?"

"Damn right I'm sure, dawg. The bitch was in the middle of the mall, letting dude tongue her ass down. I couldn't get a good look at him but from what I did see, it looked like the same dude she'd had that run in with at the club that night. Sheiiit, I would've snatched both of their asses up if we hadn't been in the middle of the mall, but we can't afford to make our shit hot, especially not because of some scandalous ass broad."

"Nah…nah…good looking, bruh. You did the right thing. I'm gonna handle her ass on my own. This shit here is personal, dawg."

I hung up the phone fuming mad, thinking of all of the shit that I would have done to her if she was in my face right now. I probably would have slit her fucking throat, but I guess GOD really does work in mysterious ways because he made sure that I was on the other side of town when I received this information so that I would have time to cool down.

I'd never felt so disrespected in my life; not even when them faggots were caught stealing from me a while back because shit like that is to be expected when you out in the streets doing wrong. "But for a muthafucka that is supposed to love you to do something so damn foul just ain't sitting well with me," I thought to myself.

This bitch had some explaining to do, and I meant that shit from the bottom of my heart. Riding through the city streets with so much on my mental, I figured that I would need a drink after this conversation that I was about to have, so I made a detour towards ABC liquor.

I searched my call log, located Sky's number and pressed send. The phone rang four times before sending me to voicemail; and while the greeting played, I thought long and hard about leaving a message but remembered that the element of surprise is a muthafucka.

Still making my way to the liquor store, I was beyond pissed off and reacting completely off of my emotions as I searched my contacts for some company. Wanting badly to call Tammy because I knew that I would literally be in for a good ride, I decided against it because she could never just gimme a lil ass and keep it moving. The bitch always wanted to cuddle and act like we a couple afterwards; and just keeping shit a hunnit, that was the last thing that I needed at that moment. I scrolled on down the list of contacts, bypassing her name until I reached Vanessa's number. I knew that she'd be down to kick it and her head game was always top notch. Come to think about it, the pussy ain't bad neither.

I nodded my head up and down before speaking aloud. "Vanessa it is," I said while pressing send on the phone.

~~~

I could hear hear my phone going off, as it played the sweet melody of "A Couple of Forevers," alerting me that Julius was calling, but at this particular moment, I could care less. Hell, I had been reaching out to his ass for the past couple of days and he'd been straight ignoring me and now all of the sudden, he has time to talk? Welp, it's just too bad that I don't have the time or the energy to deal with his shit right now, so I continued enjoying the tongue lashing that Aston was putting on my pussy as I let his call roll over to voicemail.

Yep, you heard me right. I needed this in the worst way, and I didn't think twice when I dropped my panties and allowed Aston to part my lower lips with his tongue. To hell with trying to be all that I could be for Julius if he wasn't gonna do the same for me.

Once I'd had enough, I turned around on all fours and let him enter me from behind, instantly relieving me of all of the accumulated stress from the past couple of weeks. As he glided in and out of my slippery opening, my body quivered until I reached an orgasm.

"Damn," I panted as I threw it back, matching him stroke for stoke. It felt even better than the first time. Anytime Aston and I hooked up, it was like we'd never left off. I knew that this was where I belonged, and just being honest with myself, had he never fucked up and had I never tried to get even, our asses would still be together.

"Ahhhh, shit, baby girl, I'm about to cum," he moaned as he continued to pump in and out of me. His rhythm sped up and his thrust became faster and faster. As he neared his sexual peak, he continued to ride me into ecstasy, as we climaxed together and fell back on the bed. I was in complete bliss as I lay snuggled in his arms and drifted off to sleep.

~~~

I was sleeping like a baby when I felt a strong arm wrap around me and place its hands on my protruding belly. Julius' hard body felt like a dream…a dream that I wasn't ready to wake up from so I pushed my butt out a little further so that he could spoon me how I like to be spooned and just as I started to get back into a deep sleep, he kissed me on my neck and spoke.

"I'm so glad to have you back in my life. I love you, baby girl."

My eyes bucked open and I jumped up out of the bed and rushed over to grab my clothes from the floor, tripping over my own feet in the process.

"What the hell is wrong wit' you?"

"I'm sorry," I said as I quickly threw my clothes on, and grabbed my purse and keys from the dresser. "Aston, I can't stay here. I have to go," I said hastily.

"Sky, what in the fuck are you talking about? It's three in the morning! You can't just be roaming the streets this time of morning. You're pregnant!" he yelled, getting upset.

"I gotta go...I'll call you later," I blurted out as I ran out of the room. I doubled back and stuck my head back in Aston's room door. I smiled at him as he sat in the middle of the bed still in shock, before saying, "I love you, too," and making my way out of the house and into my car.

LORD knows that I had no intentions of staying at Aston's all night long. I guess that's what happens when your partner has the magic stick. I drove in complete silence to Julius's house, thanking GOD that he'd been staying out the last few nights and hadn't had time for me because I was looking forward to going home, taking a nice, hot shower, and lying down to sleep the rest of the morning away.

When I finally made it to Julius's place, my new home away from home, everything still looked the same as I'd left it. There were no lights on and the sprinkler system was still going. That was something I often forgot to turn off and Julius hated that so I knew that he wasn't home because he would have turned it off as soon as he crossed the threshold.

I chuckled to myself, thinking of how he nitpicked over some of the smallest things at times. I parked and turned the car off. I then took my keys from the ignition, and searched the key ring for my house key, while making my way to the door.

When I entered the house, it seemed extremely cold and eerie. I even caught a chill as I made my way up the stairs and to the room. Paying the creepy feelings no attention, I made it to the room door, stuffed my keys into my purse and dropped it onto the floor as I immediately started stripping out of my clothes.

I dropped each piece of clothing into a small pile and made my way into the bathroom. When I cut the light on, I received the surprise of my life because there he was, in the flesh, sitting in the bathroom on the edge of the bathtub, in complete darkness.

"Ahhhh, shit!" I screamed, while placing my hand on my heart which was now about to beat out of my chest. "Julius, you scared the living shit outta me! Why in the hell are you sitting in here in the dark?"

Silence.

He just sat there like a mute, staring at me with dark, cold eyes, and neither of us said a word. However, I'm sure we were both silent for different reasons and I could see that much just by looking at him. He looked like he was ready to kill at any moment. Me, on the other hand, he'd scared me too short to shit, and my legs felt like they weighed a ton so I couldn't move even if I wanted to.

"Where you been?" he asked so calmly that it made me want to turn around and run. I'd seen enough movies to know that episodes like these never seemed to end well.

My legs had now started to feel like Jell-O but still I mustered up enough strength so that I could slowly start making my way back out of the bathroom, while at the same time still answering his question.

"I-I-I was at Nana's," I stuttered.

"When did you go to Nana's?" he asked, standing up from the tub and slowly advancing towards me.

"I had a doctor's appointment today and once it was over, I went to Nana's. I fell asleep and obviously lost track of time." I had become a black belt in lieology, if that is a word, or at least, I thought that I had.

Julius shook his head up and down as though he understood before continuing to speak.

"Nah, what's obvious is that your ass is lying. I called your grandma's house, Sky, and she said that she hadn't seen you since you left to come here the other day. So I'm gonna ask yo ass one mo' time, where...in...the fuck...have...you...been?" he asked with spit flying from his mouth and hatred in his eyes.

My mind was now running a marathon as I tried to search the book of lies that I usually kept stored away in my memory bank, but I kept coming up empty. I was too scared to even think straight, let alone respond. I knew that I was in deep shit and I didn't have any rope left to be pulled out.

I literally felt as though I would piss on myself at any moment. I was stuck. I'd been thrown out in the ocean, butt ass naked and without a life jacket, or at least that's how I was starting to feel as I stood there like a child being scolded and waiting impatiently for my punishment.

I dropped my head and stared at my feet. Anything to not have to look into Julius' face. As soon as I hung my head, I felt it being lifted back.

WHAM! My face was on fire as my feet left the ground and my body was tossed up into the air. It took me a minute to process exactly what had happened, but as soon as my ass landed and slid across the rug, giving me instant carpet burns, I knew then that Julius had literally tried to knock my ass into the middle of next week.

Everything happened so quickly that I don't remember ever even hollering out in pain. I was literally seeing stars. This nigga hard slapped me just that damn hard.

I looked up and saw him moving quickly across the room in my direction but I was too slow to react. As I tried my hardest to hurry and get up, I was a little too late because I felt my hair ripping from my scalp as he grabbed a handful of my beautiful mane and wrapped it around his fist.

"You been out fucking that nigga?" he asked with so much revulsion in his voice that I had to look again and make sure that his body hadn't been taken over by aliens. He didn't even sound like the same loving, caring man that I'd fallen in love with.

"Whatttt? Fucking who? I haven't been with anyone but you," I cried as both tears and snot ran down my face.

I don't know how convincing I sounded but for some reason, I just knew my ass was grass so I covered my stomach and braced myself for the ass whooping that I knew I had in store. Surprisingly it never came, at least not right then. Instead, I felt my body being slung onto the bed.

"It's funny that you would wanna try and play stupid now. Yo' ass wasn't trying to play stupid when you was all hugged up at the mall with that nigga, though!" he scolded.

I wanted to know how in the hell he knew. Had he been following me? Did someone see me? Well, at this point, it didn't even matter because before I could even attempt to put a sentence together, out of nowhere he took matters into his own hands.

WHAM! He slapped me again with the back of his hand. If I didn't know any better I would have thought that he was my pimp and I was his hoe by the way he was greasing my ass.

"You lying bitch!" he yelled. "You just won't tell the truth to save yo' life, will ya?" he asked as his hand came down again on my cheek. WHAM!

"Ahhhhhh!" I cried out in pain. I just couldn't hold it in any longer but I think that I was more in shock than anything else.

Grabbing me by my throat and bringing my face to his, he said between clenched teeth, "Bitch, shut up before I crush your muthafuckin brains in."

My body as well as my voice became paralyzed. Satisfied that I was now crying silent tears and no longer screaming, he let go of my neck and roughly pried my legs apart. "How in the hell could this sick son of a bitch be thinking about sex at a time like this?" I thought to myself as I watched him lower his face to my special place.

"So you're gonna rape me, Julius?"

He looked up at me with disgust. "Bitch, you wish... Now shut the fuck up," he scolded as he lowered his face once again.

I closed my eyes tight as I prepared myself for what was to come; but instead I felt a very light breeze across my lower lips. As I lifted my head from the bed to look down, it was then that I realized that this nigga was really on some other shit. I knew off rip that shit was about to get real as he sniffed my pussy like he was a dog in heat.

I immediately started to scoot backwards because I knew for a fact that I still smelled like Aston. Hell, the nut was still seeping out of me from earlier so I knew shit was about to go south.

"You nasty son of a bitch!" he yelled as he started raining slaps all over my face. When the blows stopped and I heard him fumbling with his belt buckle, I feared that he would really rape me now. I used that time to make a split second decision and hopped off the bed, grabbing my purse from the floor and high-tailed it out the room and down the steps. Before I could reach the bottom, Julius was on my ass like fish grease. He reached out and grabbed me by my hair again and proceeded to whip my ass...and I mean that in a literal sense.

I had no idea at first what he was whipping me with until I saw the shiny buckle as his hand went up into the air and came down, crashing on my bare flesh. When the leather from the belt connected with my ass, I couldn't help but to holler. Here I am, a grown ass woman, getting my ass tore out of the frame in a stairwell.

"I...told...you...not...to...fuck...with...me," he said as he brought the belt down, lashing me after each word.

"Ahhhhh...GODDDDD...pleaseeeeeee..."

"Shut...up...bitch!" He was swinging the belt like a mad man as he came down over and over and over again, striking me all over as I continued to holler, pray and protect my baby. "Umph," he grunted as he brought the belt down one more time.

"I'm soooo sorryyyy...Julius...pleaseeeeee," I said as I cried out for help and thought for just a moment that he had started to feel sorry for me, but quickly realized that my cries had fallen on deaf ears when he used his foot to kick me in my ass, sending me tumbling down the last few stairs.

Crawling to my knees, I tried making my way to the door but Julius had other plans for me.

"Fuck you think you going? Huh, bitch? You think you just gonna leave ah nigga now?"

WHAM! WHAM! WHAM! He was striking me like I was a nigga on the streets. I thought that real niggas usually reserved these types of ass whippings for other niggas in the street, but I was starting to feel like Princess Jasmine in the movie *Aladdin* because Julius was introducing me to a whole new world.

"You's an ole ungrateful ass hoe, you know that? Here I am, running behind you, thinking that you da truth and you ain't nothing but a hoe! Got ah nigga round here catering to yo' every need, cooking for you, taking you on shopping sprees, vacations, and introducing you to all the shit you never had; letting you into...MY WORLD...UGHH!" he yelled, kicking me in the jaw.

Falling over on my side in pain, I could barely think straight as he continued talking while I blanked in and out.

"You hoes get a good man, and don't know how to act. You wanted to have your cake and eat it too, but little do you know, you just took your last bite of this dick. Now get the fuck up and get yo ass outta here, you damn jigaboo!"

That was the last thing I heard and my precious baby boy was the last thing I thought of before I completely lost consciousness.

Chapter Eleven

MiMi

I've done did a lot of shit just to live this here lifestyle

We came straight from the bottom to the top, my lifestyle

It was the middle of the morning and my only damn day off and here Julius ass goes interrupting my fucking beauty rest. I had tried on three separate occasions to just let his calls roll to voicemail but this must have been pretty damn important because he was relentless; and I knew it was him because he was the only one in my phone with that particular ringtone. I snatched the phone off of the night stand, pressed send to answer, and immediately silenced the tunes of the music.

"Nigga, this betta be good because it's after four in the morning and you dragging a bitch up outta her sleep and shit. I shoul–"

"MiMi, shut yo punk ass up and listen for a minute!" he yelled angrily into the phone like a mad man and caught me off guard all at once. For as long as I could remember, Julius was always the one person in my family that accepted me for me, so to say that he had my undivided attention would have been an understatement.

My tone immediately softened, not only because he was my favorite cousin but because when JuJu talked, people listened…literally. Call me a bitch if you want but sheiiittt I ain't crazy so I sat up in the bed and began to listen with my ears.

"Sorry, JuJu… What's wrong, cuz?"

JuJu was in a state of panic and I could tell that he needed my help. I could hear it in his voice, but I still remained silent until I could find out exactly what was going on and what in the hell he needed my help with at damn near five o'clock in the morning.

"Cuz, I fucked up...I fucked up bad," he said while sounding distressed and out of breath.

"What's wrong, cuz? You're scaring me."

"I don't know what's wrong, MiMi, but shit is all fucked up. How quick can you get here?"

Being the person that I am, I put my beauty rest on the back burner and replied before hanging up the phone, "Cuz, I'm throwing on my clothes right now. I'll be there as soon as I can."

When I pulled up to Julius's house, the gate was wide open, and that wasn't like him at all. He usually ran a really tight ship and to be slipping like this was definitely a sign that something really terrible had happened. I parked my car in the driveway behind Skyla's car, hopped out and ran up to the door. I proceeded to knock, but the door was already slightly open.

Now I was really shitting bricks because I'd seen enough movies to know that this usually meant that somebody was about to die, and if they had to choose between me, him, and Skyla's old blackanese ass, then I knew that I'd probably be the first to go. Hell, all black women in the movies usually died first. Yep, I said it. Black women.

With that in mind, I stepped back off of the porch and sprinted back to my car, unlocking the door, and leaning in to retrieve my trusty hot pink .22 from the glove box.

When I made my way back to the front door, I slowly eased it open with my gun drawn. I didn't see anything suspicious right off, and that could have been because it was dark as hell in the house with the exception of the light upstairs shining down from the staircase.

"Julius?" I called out, but there was no answer. I silently started to pray. "Oh GOD, please don't let me die in this bitch," I said aloud while fanning myself.

It had been a minute since I'd been to Julius' house so I couldn't remember where the light switch was in the foyer, but I remembered where the dining room light was located so I quietly made my over to the dining room area and flipped on the light switch.

Now making my way to the staircase, I could finally see a figure on the ground that was laying slightly to the right side of the staircase and my heart dropped at the thought that something bad happening to my favorite cousin. I broke out in a full sprint while hollering and screaming for Julius.

"Juliussss! Juliussss! What happened to youuuuuuu?" I cried as I dropped on my knees turning the body over.

I gasped while placing my hand over my mouth. What I saw turned my damn stomach. I was not at all prepared to see my girl Sky laying in a pool of blood, looking as though she'd been beaten into a bloody pulp. My eyes immediately traveled down to her belly and my heart ached. I said another prayer, but this time for her and her unborn child.

I was now in full-blown panic mode as I cried over her limp body while looking at her once beautiful face. It was now black and blue and looked as though she'd been in a fight with Mike Tyson in his prime. She even had various lashes and bruises all over her naked body. Her hair was disheveled and her eyes were closed shut and stained with dried up tears.

I put my face to hers trying to see if I could hear her breathe, but there was nothing. I then picked up her arm from the floor and examined her wrist, placing my fingers there to search for a pulse as I had seen people do so many times in the movies.

"Ahhhhhh! There is a GOD!" I yelled once I discovered a pulse. It was barely there. Nevertheless, she had one and that meant that there was hope.

I then remembered that you're never supposed to move a person when they're hurt, at least that's what I'd been told. But trying to wait for an ambulance to find out where JuJu's place was located would definitely be a death wish because this nigga stayed way out in west bubba fuck. Besides, being that this is the crime scene, I figured that wouldn't be a good look anyhow.

Taking my chances, I tucked my gun away and used my strength to pick up a naked Sky. I cradled her in my arms and took her out to my car, carefully laying her in the back seat on top of my jacket. I then hopped in my car and took off.

I placed my hazard lights on because this was definitely a state of an emergency and I had no intentions of stopping at any lights. My girl was in trouble and she needed me in the worst way. As I breezed through the streets on my way to the hospital, I grabbed my phone and called Julius. He picked up on the first ring, like he'd been waiting for my call, and before I could say anything, he started talking.

"Just get my baby some help, cuz, and make sure that you tell her I only did that because I love her."

I took the phone from my ear and my screen indicated that the call was no longer active. I tried calling back and the nigga sent me to voicemail.

"Aaarrrrggghhhh! That sick son of a bitch!" I yelled to no one in particular.

I dreaded making my next call, but I had to do it. It was the only way that Sky's grandparents would know what was going on. I mean, they raised her so they definitely should have that right.

I picked up the phone and called Raye.

"Damn, MiMi... This shit couldn't have waited until the roosters stopped crowing?" she asked groggily into the phone.

"Hell no, bitch! Sky's has been hurt! I'm on my way to the hospital with her. Meet me at Orlando Regional

Medical Center, ASAP!" I spoke quickly into the phone before hanging up.

I really had no other choice since I knew that she would want to ask a ton of questions for which I had no real answers. I also knew that I could count on her to call and tell Sky's grandparents as well. She would do that without me even having to tell her. She was just that good of a friend, always had been.

I looked back into the backseat to see that Skyla hadn't moved from the position that I'd placed her in.

"LORD, please don't let her die on me....please don't let her die on me..." was all that I could chant for the rest of the drive to the hospital.

Chapter Twelve

Sky

I woke to the sound of beeping and all of my loved ones standing over me. MiMi was here, Aston was here and it looked as though he'd even been crying, Rayne was sitting in a chair next to my bed while Nana and Granddaddy stood over me praying for strength and healing. Nia was even standing at my bedside, holding my hand.

Had I died and gone to heaven and GOD let my loved ones come with me? Then it dawned on me. I didn't see Julius anywhere. Where was he? Was I dreaming?

Hearing MiMi's voice made me realize that I definitely wasn't dreaming.

"Look! She's awake!" I heard someone yell.

All eyes were focused on me as Raye hopped up from the chair like a jack-in-the-box, ran out of the room, and yelled for a nurse.

"What's going on?" I managed to ask. My throat was dry as hell and it hurt too bad to talk. I needed something to drink…and fast.

"Shhhh... It's okay, baby," Nia said as she rubbed my cheek. "Everything is going to be alright."

I could barely feel her touch so I knew that she wasn't touching me to hurt me, but my face was in so much pain. Hell, my whole body was in pain. I needed some answers and I needed them now.

I looked up at Nana and Granddaddy and they had smiles on their faces wider than the Red Sea, and then there was Aston. He looked like he was ready to strike and kill. I couldn't place where his anger was coming from, though. I still didn't have any answers and from the looks of things, Nia didn't want me to even try to talk right now.

"Well, good morning, beautiful. I'm your nurse, Amy, and I'll be taking care of you. You gave us quite the scare, young lady," she said with a great smile on her face. "I'm just going to take your vitals and then I can get you something to drink because I bet you're thirsty, huh?"

Everyone stepped back to give Amy her space and she quickly did her job; and keeping true to her promise, not only did she send me a cup of water but also a little cup of apple juice.

My mom poked a hole into the top of the apple juice using the straw that Amy had left for me and brought the straw to my lips so that I could drink. At first, the cold fluid hurt a little bit going down, but after a few sips, I was okay.

"So, is anyone going to tell me what I'm doing here?"

Silence.

Raye stepped in front of me and reached into her purse, pulling out a small compact mirror. While I was wondering what she was going to do with it, she opened it and positioned it in my face so that I could see the beast staring back at me. I didn't comment. I just looked and stared, cried and stared some more.

"Sky, you don't remember anything that happened to you?" she asked as she continued to hold the mirror steady for me to see myself.

After seeing myself and glancing around the room once more and seeing that Julius still hadn't made it to my side, the slides started to replay in my head like a bad movie.

I could remember everything from the time that I cut on the bathroom light until the time he told me to get the fuck out of his house. Tears silently cascaded down my face. I was embarrassed to my core. You would've thought that everyone was watching the trailer in my head as well.

Everyone gathered around, rubbing me and telling me that things would be okay and how it wasn't my fault but I knew that it was. If only I hadn't stepped out on him, I would have never been in this situation.

I cried for the old and the new. I cried for fucked up endings and wishful beginnings. I even cried knowing that Nia was making an effort by being here with me.

"How long have I been here?" I ask.

"A little over a week, pumpkin," Granddaddy answered.

"A week?"

"Yes, baby. A week," Nia responded.

"The doctors say that you'd slipped into a coma, and no one knew how long you'd be in that condition," Raye stated.

"I'm just glad you're okay, baby girl," Aston said as he walked over and placed a loving kiss on my forehead.

I just sat there like a mute, listening and taking everything in.

"The doctor said that there is a possibility that you may have a bit of memory loss whenever you did come to; but not to worry because it was normal. He also said that there is a possibility that things may come back to your memory in small parts. Do you remember me bringing you here?" MiMi asked.

I shook my head no.

"Do you remember anything before blacking out?"

I nodded my head yes as more tears escaped the slits of my eyes.

"Everything…I remember everything…" I said almost above a whisper.

"Well, we need to know everything, ma. It's really important," Aston said while pleading with me with his eyes for the information.

As I replayed the story back just as I remembered it, not sparing any details, I could see everybody's face start to wear a scowl, MiMi's included.

I then placed my hand on my belly hoping that I'd succeeded in protecting my baby and realized that my stomach was neither as big nor hard as it should have been. It was empty and I immediately started to panic. I was in a state of shock and I needed for my baby to be okay.

"Where's my baby?" I yelled. "What happened to my baby? Oh GOD, please let my baby be okay…" I cried as I broke down, releasing the flood gates of heaven from my eyes.

Aston walked over and sat on the bed next to me. Rubbing my back and letting me cry everything out. "Baby girl, he's okay. They had to do an emergency C-section on you the night you got here. The baby was in distress and his heart rate kept dropping. They didn't want to risk anything so they took the baby. He was born a little early but other than that, he's fine. He has all of his fingers and toes, a clean bill of health and he's just as handsome as can be," he relayed with a smile.

I smiled through my tears as Aston talked about the baby. I could see the excitement rolling off of him in waves as he spoke about the baby.

"How big was he?"

"He was 5 pounds and 13 inches long. I named him after me. I hope that was okay. You were unresponsive and they needed to have a name for the birth certificate."

"No...no...that's fine."

"Can you believe that my mama even came to see him? That was a shocker for me and Rayne because you know she doesn't ever have time to do anything that doesn't revolve around her," he chuckled.

I was shocked but grateful that a gift so small could be a gift so big. Everyone just sat around looking and smiling as Aston talked to me about Jr. "Baby girl, he has your hair and eyes, but everything else is me," he said with confidence.

"Is that right?" I asked sarcastically. "When can I see him?"

"Me and Granddaddy are gonna go get some rest, and let you catch up with your new bundle of joy. Besides, we have to get Ty from the sitter. I'll let the nurse know that you want to see the baby. We'll talk to you later," she said as she and Granddaddy bent down simultaneously to kiss my cheeks, one on each side.

"Okay, thank you, Nana. And kiss Ty for me."

While waiting for the baby to be brought in, everyone started to make their exits. Rayne promised to come back later on and Nia even promised to return after she went home to shower and eat. She didn't know it, but her being with me meant the world to me. I finally had my mommy back.

When MiMi got ready to make her exit, she told me that she would call me later to see if I needed anything before she came back.

"MiMi, I just want to say thank you."

"Sky, you know you my bitch. You don't have to thank me, because I know that you would have done the same thing for me. I love you like a sister, boo," she said with tears in her eyes.

I had no reply except, "I love you, too, MiMi."

She and I never mentioned Julius again during my hospital stay and I was okay with that. I knew that she felt partly responsible for his actions but it wasn't her fault. That nigga knew exactly what he was doing.

The only people left in the room now were Aston and I. We sat and chatted until the nurse came rolling Junior in. When she took him out of the hospital baby bed and placed him in my arms, I fell in love all over again. I would have never guessed in a million years that I could love someone how I'd just fallen in love. It was love at first sight and he'd swept me off my feet without even doing anything. Junior looked up at me with his little slanted greenish-brown eyes and my heart melted. If ever I had a reason to keep pushing, this would be it.

It was just me, Aston and Junior against the world. In so many words, without really even using any words, I knew that Aston would be here for the long haul and for once in my life, I felt complete. I was no longer empty or searching for love, I'd found all the love that I would ever need right here within these four walls.

Chapter Thirteen

Aston

It had been about three months since baby girl's run-in with dude and let her tell it, she hadn't heard from him since. I probably wouldn't have believed her had I not been the one to take her to get her car from his house.

I had to admit, dude was living large. It was just too bad he hadn't been able to enjoy the luxury of his home over the last few months. His ass had been missing in action, but I had been watching his shit night and day. I mean, any time I had a little bit of free time from Sky and Jr., I was at this nigga's shit waiting on him to slip up and come home, but hadn't had any luck.

Tonight was no different. When I got ready to leave the house, I kissed baby girl and Jr., told them how much I loved them and made my way outside to my car. I made it a point to kiss her and tell her how much they meant to me and how much I loved them every time I left the house because I never knew if it would be my last.

Getting revenge on Julius had become like an obsession. I felt that since I wasn't around to protect her when it happened, I had to make sure that I made his ass pay for what happened. The ultimate price in my book was his life. So I was either gonna blow his fucking brains out or go out trying.

I was on a mission and a mission it was as I made my way to Julius' home to wait on his arrival. I had gotten so good that I'd turned the almost hour drive into a mere 36 minute ride. I'd scoped out the area and even found little shortcuts to his house.

When I made it to my destination, I parked my car at the end of the trail in the nearby woods, grabbed my Glock 40 and made sure that my trusty .380 was strapped to my ankle. Dressed from head to toe in all black, I pulled the black ski mask down, you could never be too careful, and made my way through the wooded area. I climbed the tree across the street from his house and waited for my target to show, just as I had every night for the past three months.

I had been in the tree for close to three hours when I decided that dude's ole punk ass wasn't gonna show. Just as I started to descend from my post, I was caught off guard by a pair of headlights turning in the estate.

Julius

It had been some time since I'd been home. I'd been in the Big Apple laying low, but felt that it was time to return to the new home that I'd made for myself in Orlando.

I hadn't reached out to anyone, not even MiMi. She'd been calling me non-stop, cursing me out from A to Z on my voicemail about what I'd done to her friend. Hell, her friend wasn't worried about me when she was slanging mud on my name out in these streets, giving my pussy away for free and tonguing niggas down for the whole world to see.

Nope, I still had no remorse for what I'd done to Sky because I'd already told her ass not to fuck me over and she did just that. I loved her and she shitted on me. I promised that I would never let another woman take me to that point, but that is exactly what she did.

"She better be lucky that I still had a little bit of love for her because if not, her ass would have made the news like the last bitch I was with...baby and all," I thought to myself. I'd told Skyla that my last relationship ended because ole girl got shot in a drive-by.

"But shit what was I supposed to tell her? That I killed the bitch because she was stealing from me? Bitches just ain't shit. You give 'em the world and that still ain't enough," I said to myself as I made my way to the front door and let myself in.

It was dark out so I couldn't see anything but when I walked in, I was hit with the smell of stale blood. Blood that had probably stained my tile because of Sky's ole trifling ass. I hit the light switch so that I could make my way upstairs, but nothing happened. I knew that I'd paid the light bill and I just felt in my gut that something wasn't right.

I immediately took my .9mm from the small of my back and started to clear the house from top to bottom. Once I'd made sure that the inside was clear, I made my way outside to the breaker box.

Aston

I crouched down behind the shrub on the side of the house, waiting for Julius' ole punk ass to come out to check the breaker so that I could make my way inside the house.

Like clockwork, the nigga rounded the corner with his gun drawn but looked in only one direction. Once he started to make his way to the breaker, I made a run for it. Crossing the threshold in the foyer, I quickly made my way upstairs and hid behind the couch on the second floor. I was sure to be as quiet as possible and as still as a nail.

I could hear dude come into the house and saw the lights immediately start to come on. I stayed hidden, waiting patiently for my target to come into view.

My adrenaline was pumping, my hands were sweaty and my blood was boiling as I thought about my beautiful baby girl and how she looked laid up in that hospital bed a few months back. It was like everything had just happened. Her bruises were so vivid in my mind that they could have been a painted there.

After about twenty minutes of waiting, Julius finally started to make his way upstairs and, lucky for me, he was on the phone and not paying attention to his surroundings. I bet this nigga thought that he would be safe in the presence of his own home, huh? And to make matters worse, this nigga hard the nerve to be on the phone talking to some bitch when he'd left my bitch for dead. Oh yeah, he had the game all fucked up.

As he started to make his way up to the third floor, I quickly emerged from behind the couch and hit him in the back of the head with the butt of my gun.

"Uggghhhh," he growled as his phone went flying one way and his ass fell face first to the floor.

"Arrgghhhhhh!" I yelled as I immediately sent a couple of kicks to his rib cage. "Fuck…nigga…So…I…hear…that…you…like…to…put …your…hands…on…women…huh?" I yelled, questioning him as I sent kicks to his rib cage, never letting up or giving him a chance to retaliate.

I could see that he was in pain and definitely caught off guard, so in no way was he in any shape to be able to fight back, and I was okay with that. He'd beaten my woman until she was damn near unrecognizable and left not only her, but my son for dead. This nigga had to be out of his rabbit ass mind if he thought for one second that I felt any remorse for him.

I watched as he balled himself into a fetal position, closing his eyes and trying to fight through the pain; but I wanted him to see who was on the delivering end of each kick that was being delivered to his ass.

"Turn yo monkey ass over," I said as I removed my ski-mask while standing over him and cocking my gun.

Slowly but surely, he turned over, looking a bloody mess. He smiled, displaying a mouth full of bloody teeth. I guessed that was from his fall. Either way, I didn't give a damn.

"So…we meet again, huh?" he asked, smiling. "Do you have any idea who you're fucking with?"

"Damn right I do, but obviously you don't, because if you did, you'd know that you're in a realllll shitty situation right now," I said, smiling back at him.

"You do a lot of talking for a bitch that's supposed to be working with a royal flush."

"No worries. I just wanted to make sure you knew who'd be responsible for you taking your last breath. I was always taught to look ah nigga in the eyes before I kill him," I said seriously.

"Fuck you, nigga! Kill me…and tell ya bitch I'll see her and that bastard ass baby of hers in hell, pussy!"

"Lights out, bitch!"

BLAOW! BLAOW! I let my nine sound off, damn near blowing his entire face off. There was blood and brain matter all over the staircase and walls. It looked like something out of a horror movie.

I would have loved to have tortured him first, but the last comment he'd made did something to me and I wanted to make sure that he swallowed those words.

I quickly remembered what had just taken place and, although we were out in the middle of nowhere and I'd enjoyed playing GOD with his worthless life, I didn't want to risk being caught. I had a family to get home to.

I quickly tucked my gun into the small of my back and made my way out the same way that I'd come in…quietly and undetected.

Chapter Fourteen

Sky

Eight Months Later

I was sitting on the back porch of my new house, watching Junior play on his swing set as Rayne and I made plans for his first birthday. I couldn't believe he'd be turning one next month. Boy, how time flies.

It had been almost a year since Julius had left me for dead and I couldn't have been happier to have survived that whole ordeal.

Before, I felt that I had nothing to live for, but as I reflect on all of my newfound blessings, I couldn't help but to beg to differ. Aston and I had just recently received the paternity results confirming that Junior was 99.999 percent his son. That was the best house warming gift we'd received by far.

Aston and I have been rocking ever since my accident, and just recently moved into a house not far from Nana's so that we could do the whole family thing. My man was officially a one woman man.

Nana and Granddaddy were still raising Tyler but Nia was now staying with them and playing a more active role in his life. She and I had even made up. She'd been here with us every step of the way since the hospital, and I was proud to say that she hadn't missed one holiday, birthday or special event yet. She was still attending her NA meetings religiously and I thought that those were really helping with her sobriety these days.

Rayne and B were still going strong and were now talking about "taking their relationship to the next level," whatever the hell that meant.

Mimi had been looking for Julius for months on end and after she continuously called him with no answer and his phone eventually saying that the number had been disconnected, she called the police to file a missing persons report and even put her ear to the streets. It wasn't until about four months ago that Julius was found dead in his home. MiMi was devastated. She'd shut everyone out and had become a recluse. I really felt bad for her because they were always so close. They didn't have a funeral for him because he didn't have much family. I don't think that I would have attended, just out of respect for Aston, but I'd long ago forgiven him because I know that deep down inside, if he really wanted to, he could have killed me. So even though he and I didn't work out, I would have never wished for him to lose his life. I mean, there was a point in time where I really did love him. We'd had some good times and great memories, and for that, I will always love him. I just wished that I could have my girl MiMi back. I really missed having her around. Maybe she'd come around soon.

I tuned back in to Raye to finish the details for Junior's first birthday bash, after silently giving thanks to GOD for giving me a reason to press on.

Being unhappy was now a thing of the past. I had finally found my way, in life that is. And most importantly, I'd found MY FOREVER PIECE.

ABOUT THE AUTHOR

My name is Carnisha but I use the pen name Nisha L. I am currently in school seeking my degree in Criminal Justice and Sociology but in the midst of my busy schedule, I always find time to write.

Writing is my first passion as I was inspired to write at a very young age by my mother who did a lot of poetry writing and skits. She would write for churches, school plays and personal use; even earning a few awards in the process.

I was so intrigued by her ability to bring characters and scenes to life through a pen and paper that I followed in her footsteps. I started off writing poetry and as I got older, the need to share with the world my talent through story became inevitable.

Writing is something that I love to do and I hope that you all enjoy these beautiful works of Urban Fiction that I am creating for years to come; because I plan to be around for a very long time!

OTHER WORKS

Temptations
Publications
****

NOW accepting submissions for

URBAN FICTION & STREET LIT!!!!

If you have a **FINISHED** manuscript and think that you have

what it takes to become a part of the team,

email your submission(s) to:

tpubsubmissions@gmail.com

or, mail to:

Temptations Publications Inc.

P.O. Box 694534

Miami, Florida 33269

Be sure to include:

AT LEAST the first **THREE** chapters of your manuscript,

Your name (and pen name if applicable), Phone #, Address,

Bio & Synopsis

We look forward to working with you.

L., NISHA

www.ingramcontent.com/pod-product-compliance
Lightning Source LLC
LaVergne TN
LVHW011331080426
835513LV00006B/279